AMERICA'S RIGHT TURN

For the Roper Family:

Best Wishes,

Bill Berman

April 15, 1994

The American Moment
Stanley I. Kutler, Series Editor

America's Right Turn

From Nixon to Bush

WILLIAM C. BERMAN

The Johns Hopkins University Press

Baltimore and London

In Memory of My Father and Mother
Samuel and Esther Berman

The Johns Hopkins University Press
2715 North Charles Street
Baltimore, Maryland 21219-4319

Library of Congress Cataloging-in-Publication Data

Berman, William C., 1932–
    America's right turn : from Nixon to Bush / William C. Berman.
        p.   cm. — (The American moment)
    Includes bibliographical references and index.
    ISBN 0-8018-4825-3 (alk. paper). — ISBN 0-8018-4826-1 (pbk. : alk. paper)
    1. Conservatism—United States—History—20th century. 2. United States—
Politics and government—1945–1989. 3. United States—Politics and government—
1989–1993. 4. United States—Social conditions—1960–1980.   I. Title.   II. Series.
E839.5.B44   1994
973.92—dc20   93-38003

A catalog record of this book is available from the British Library.

In the present crisis, government is not the solution to our problem, government is the problem.

—Ronald Reagan's first Inaugural Address, January 20, 1981

In the 1960s, the liberals were widely seen as having failed to deal with major questions of law enforcement, taxation, fiscal management, and the role of government as well as race. They were repudiated and the Republicans moved into a 25-year period of executive hegemony. Twelve years of Reagan and Bush has not cured the problems, either. It hasn't given us morning in America. It's produced more columns of smoke rising from our inner cities.

—Kevin Phillips, *New York Times*, May 2, 1992

Contents

FOREWORD

The lingering trauma of Vietnam, together with the disruptive dynamics of a new global economic system and heightened social tensions at home, fractured the long-dominant liberal coalition in the United States. The result was the political ascendancy of a new conservative majority; it was, as William Berman aptly describes it in this pioneering study, "America's Right Turn."

Ideology, of course, is important, and Berman duly acknowledges the content of competing political appeals. But he also carefully analyzes the social and economic considerations that propel ideology. Berman recognizes, for example, that the inflation of the 1970s provides a more concrete explanation for public attitudes than any mystical conservative rationalization of the magic of the marketplace. He understands, too, that the conservative triumph had important roots in the politics of race, opposition to the "rights revolution," and the globalization of the American economy.

The New Deal coalition that had dominated American politics and values since the 1930s floundered in the 1970s. However real or imagined their grievances, people found government—big, interventionist, and tax-consuming—a convenient scapegoat. The traditional conservative appeal for diminished government struck a responsive chord as Americans reeled from inflation, high taxes, and racial tensions. Meanwhile, for the first time in more than three decades, many Americans began to experience a decline in economic well-being. Ronald Reagan indeed "struck the political equivalent of gold," as Berman writes, when he promised to get government off the backs of people. Yet government hardly diminished in the 1980s. We had the anomaly of antitax dogma as an article of political faith, while political leaders continued to promise everything for nothing. During the Reagan-Bush years, tax and fiscal policies resulted in a spectacular rise in the national debt. That, in turn, reduced American economic power and influence abroad and paralyzed any efforts to fund programs to combat heightened social problems. Ironically—perhaps fittingly—the economic issues that fueled the conservative triumph led to a decline in fortunes and George Bush's defeat in 1992.

The years of conservative dominance reflected a fear of rapid, pervasive change in people's lives. With the cold war over, with America's powerful political and economic hegemony challenged by new economic powers, not military ones, Americans felt adrift and apprehensive. Rising prosperity and affluence no longer could be taken for granted. Jobs, savings, and pensions seemed precarious; dominant social mores and hierarchical patterns had been transformed as women and minority groups made dramatic advances in their lives. Quite naturally, people adversely affected by these developments retreated into nostalgia for what they believed had been a better day. The "gridlock" in governance mirrored the frustration and uncertainty in the lives of many ordinary Americans. By 1992, the conservative appeal appeared exhausted as the presidential election signaled deep dissatisfaction with the pervasive stalemate in the economy as well as in government. But what remained unclear, as Berman concludes, was whether Clinton's triumph in that election could overcome the "complex legacy of liberalism's past defeat or conservatism's recent political triumph." For now, at least, we can appreciate Berman's informed, insightful account of that legacy.

STANLEY I. KUTLER

ACKNOWLEDGMENTS

This project was kept on track thanks to the wise counsel and guidance of Stanley Kutler, the editor of the American Moment series. He knew the story and gave me an opportunity to tell it. Henry Tom, executive editor of the Johns Hopkins University Press, provided excellent advice at a critical juncture. Carol Ehrlich, senior manuscript editor at the Johns Hopkins University Press, improved the overall quality of the manuscript. My colleagues Robert Accinelli, John Cairns, and Richard Sandbrook pointed me in the right direction. Professors Jacob Vander Meulen and David Sheinin, good friends and able historians, helped in many important ways. Professor Jacque Berger was always a receptive listener. Needless to say, I alone am responsible for what appears in this book.

As always, my family was with me from beginning to end. My wife, Debbie, worked hard to improve my syntax. My daughter, Rachel, blessed with infinite patience, showed me how to operate a computer. My son, Daniel, was a constant source of encouragement as well as a careful reader. And our family cats, Samantha and Mingus, kept me company while I worked on this manuscript.

AMERICA'S RIGHT TURN

Introduction

Ronald Reagan's election as president of the United States produced a seismic shift in the political balance of power in the country. Conservatism, helped enormously by the earlier collapse of the New Deal order, had at last made it into the promised land of power in 1980.

In order to explain conservatism's rise and triumph, this work presents an analysis of presidential politics that links a form of social history to political history for the purpose of casting light on the specific character of American political culture at a given point in time. That is, politics became the medium by which the great cultural and racial upheavals of the sixties and seventies were eventually absorbed into the political system for the benefit of a powerful new conservative establishment. And the key to the legitimation of that establishment was the winning of the presidency, the solar plexus of the American political and constitutional system.

The rightward shift reflected a new reality. Liberalism had become a pejorative word for millions of voters, who still supported many of the social and economic programs of the Democratic party. But they opposed the cultural and social agenda of left liberalism, as it was represented by the McGovern movement and the Supreme Court. Liberalism, in their view, had become a vehicle for big governmental spending programs for blacks. At the same time, the Supreme Court's "rights revolution" seemed more concerned with protecting, in the words of journalist Harold Myerson, "the one against the many—*not the many against the powerful.*" Such was the perception of many once-loyal working-class Democrats, who now turned against the party and program of "limousine liberalism."

Significantly, liberalism had delivered no such mixed message for a majority of voters in the thirties and forties. At the heart of New Deal liberalism was a fragile social contract that had been negotiated between the federal government and the citizens of the United States in the name of the general welfare. This was Franklin Roosevelt's legacy to his fellow Democrats, who in turn benefited from and were helped by the modest welfare state that his administration created. New Dealers implemented policies and programs designed to alleviate widespread economic suffering, believing that the federal government had a responsibility to protect citizens from those aspects of the business cycle which produced large-scale unemployment and economic hardship.

Democrats had also won organized labor's friendship by supporting its right to pursue collective bargaining agreements. And for having sponsored social legislation, such as Social Security and the GI Bill of Rights, they had received the votes of millions of immigrants residing in the big urban centers of the North, as well as many others living in the small towns and rural communities of the South. At the same time, Democrats had moved to strengthen the regulatory powers of the federal government, embraced Keynesian fiscal policies, and used monetary mechanisms to help stimulate economic growth. During and after World War II, powerful interests from business and finance supported these initiatives as good public policy. For nearly forty years, this program was the basis for sectional cooperation and class harmony that allowed the Democratic party to forge a national political majority out of otherwise divergent minorities and competing interest groups.

Conservatives were outraged by those institutional arrangements, which constituted the heart of New Deal and Fair Deal liberalism. Seeing in them a threat to individual liberty and to freedom of the marketplace, they believed that the creation of the welfare state was the first step on the "road to serfdom." Later, a sophisticated conservative thinker like Frank Meyer fused their antistatist ideology and moral traditionalism with a militant anticommunism. Thus when Senator Barry Goldwater made his bid for the presidency in 1964, he operated from a conservative "vital center," which reflected Meyer's ideological construct of the fifties. Although Goldwater was soundly defeated, his campaign, along with Governor George Wallace's subsequent attack on the power and values of the liberal establishment, helped prepare the way for the great shift in national political beliefs and attitudes that culminated in Ronald Reagan's election in 1980.

As the meaning of liberalism was transformed by the events of the sixties and seventies, so too were the politics of conservatism. Responding to the cultural upheaval of the times, a conservative New Right and a New Religious Right now emerged as a growing force in the ranks of the Republican party, especially in the Sunbelt. They helped to produce a groundswell of support across the country for the politics of family values, patriotism, and fighting crime, issues that the Republicans had exploited since 1968. As Lee Atwater, an astute Republican tactician of the Reagan and Bush administrations, well understood, the key to the party's success lay in redirecting populist resentment of the rich toward a governmental establishment that supported a liberal social and cultural agenda. The "trick," he suggested, was to choose "those social issues that do not alienate the country clubbers, since, again, we need their votes and the populists' to win in the South."

Although the emergence of conservative populism played a key role in helping to undermine the New Deal order, the changing position of business vis-à-vis government was at least as important. By the late seventies, business was faced with a serious challenge to its hegemony and profits as a result of globalized competition. Consequently, employing good organization and a unified strategy, it pressured Congress into weakening several of the regulatory reforms of the late sixties and early seventies, and reducing corporate taxes as well.

Once the backlash against the "rights revolution" converged with the tax revolt of the late seventies and that powerful business mobilization, the ideas and ideology of big government liberalism, epitomized by Hubert Humphrey, quickly lost their attraction for a majority of voters. The stage was now set for Ronald Reagan, that master of symbolic politics, to provide the glue that solidified an otherwise shaky and unstable conservation coalition into a presidential majority.

As America turned right, so did other Western democracies. Conservative politicians also took power in Britain, West Germany, and Canada, promising to produce economic growth via deregulated markets and, in some cases, lower taxes. That message appealed to large numbers of middle-class voters on both sides of the Atlantic Ocean, especially at a time when American liberalism and European social democracy were in a state of political and economic crisis due to their inability to reduce inflation or to cope with a stagnating economy.

Like other conservative triumphs, then, Reagan's election proved that politics and ideology matter in determining who gets what and why. But so does the economy. A leitmotif of this study is that political outcomes, more often than not, are shaped by economic circumstances and conditions that transcend in importance a cluster of "social issues." Intense social, cultural, and racial conflicts moved American presidential politics to the populist right after the late sixties, caused by a crisis that liberalism could not resolve or transcend. It was, however, the presence of persistent inflation and the changes wrought at home by the process of globalization that exacerbated those conflicts and elected Ronald Reagan in 1980. Social issues helped Reagan win a landslide victory in 1984, but it was a downturn in the inflation rate and an upturn in the economy that clinched his reelection. George Bush's manipulation of racial politics, coupled with his pledge not to raise taxes, gave him an opportunity to win the presidency in 1988. But he was assisted by a favorable economic climate, which in turn prevented Michael Dukakis from exploiting the one big issue he needed to overcome his reputation as a social and cultural "liberal."

Reagan's deficit trap also made it difficult for the Democrats to move in a different direction. When Reagan ran for the White House in 1980, he promised the American people jobs and prosperity via supply-side economics. Thus did the "economics of joy," in the words of economist Herbert Stein, triumph over the politics of limits. But eventually the bill for Reaganomics came due, amounting to trillions of dollars in new governmental, corporate, and consumer debt, along with a massive increase in the federal deficit. Reagan's huge spending programs and tax cuts locked the Democrats into playing the politics of austerity. Afraid of the voters' wrath, they could ill afford to be seen as "tax and spend" Democrats, or supporters of expensive new programs designed to help urban America. Such was the extent of conservatism's triumph over liberalism as the decade of the nineties began that without a serious economic downturn, political efforts to renew Franklin Roosevelt's social contract were doomed to fail.

The Politics of Culture
and Class, 1964–1974

The 1964 presidential election was ideologically charged like few others in recent American political history, as President Lyndon Johnson, a centrist liberal of the New Deal persuasion, faced Senator Barry Goldwater, a Republican conservative from Arizona. Given those choices, Johnson's vast experience in government and his political maturity proved to be reassuring to millions of Americans, especially in the aftermath of John Kennedy's assassination in Dallas. Consequently, he scored a massive victory, winning 61 percent of the popular vote and a landslide in the electoral college while defending the liberal status quo from a radical conservative who wanted to abolish Social Security and who threatened to use nuclear weapons in Vietnam.

Yet, despite the liberal euphoria that was created in the aftermath of LBJ's victory, there was another side to the story that many liberals failed to see. Goldwater not only won twenty-seven million votes across the country, he also established a beachhead for the Republican party in the South by winning five states. Although Goldwater himself was no racist, his candidacy attracted strong support in the region because he opposed the Kennedy-Johnson civil rights bills, and because he denounced the social programs of the Washington liberal establishment. Outside the South, a number of Goldwater's social views, whether on the subject of welfare spending or the recent Supreme Court decision to take prayer out of the public schools, probably resonated with many more voters than those who ended up supporting him. In a different political environment, those particular issues had the potential to play a much bigger part in deciding political outcomes than was the case in 1964.

Meanwhile, Lyndon Johnson's victory that year provided him and the Democratic party with a unique opportunity to legislate his vision of a Great Society in America. Under Johnson's direction and leadership, the welfare state, for a brief period, was extended and enlarged, as his consensus encompassed the pressing political and economic needs of the urban poor, the elderly, and the racial minorities. Thanks, then, to a newly established mandate for reform, the federal government provided funding for social programs designed to reach people not covered by New Deal legislation of an earlier era.

Unfortunately for President Johnson and the Democratic party, their effort to bring formerly marginalized groups into American society via the politics of inclusion failed to offer much to ordinary voters, who did not derive direct benefits from poverty programs, civil rights legislation, or even Medicare unless they were over sixty-five. Unlike the New Deal, with its class-based and universalized programs, the Great Society lacked a broader appeal; so its success depended very much on Johnson's ability and skill in avoiding the alienation of large blocs of voters who did not necessarily want those programs he proposed and whose tax dollars would have to pay for them.

Although the Great Society achieved real, albeit limited, success in ameliorating certain basic racial and economic inequities that had chronically plagued American society, its dynamism and momentum were soon undercut by the changing political situation inside the country. A white backlash, resulting from fear of urban disorder and opposition to open housing, helped to revive the Republican party in 1966. Many working-class whites of ethnic background, though nominally Democratic, now held Lyndon Johnson and the Democrats responsible for encouraging those unwanted developments; so they, along with other voters, expressed their anger by sending forty-seven more Republicans to the House of Representatives. This result effectively destroyed Johnson's liberal majority in the House, which had been based on a key bloc of northern Democrats; their ranks were seriously depleted in the election of 1966.

That volatile domestic scene was also ready-made for exploitation by Governor George Wallace of Alabama, a skillful political demagogue whose powerful stump speaking style attracted widespread attention. Building on Barry Goldwater's 1964 attack on the welfare state, defense of limited government, and opposition to the liberal civil rights agenda, he played to his audience's resentment, if not hatred, of militant blacks, student radicals, and, above all, the eastern establishment. His was a potent message that damned the federal government for creating the country's troubles. Because many white voters across the country liked what Wallace said, he soon emerged as a political threat to the national Democratic party's continuing hold on power and as a serious rival to the Republicans as well.

While Wallace geared up for the 1968 election, Lyndon Johnson was faced with a deadlock in Vietnam and growing racial tension and cultural conflict at home. On March 30, 1968, Johnson, with his once-formidable coalition now shattered, took himself out of the race, leaving the door open to dovish senators Eugene McCarthy and Robert Kennedy to challenge Vice-President Hubert Humphrey for the party's presidential nomination. But the assassination of Senator Kennedy in early June foreclosed matters, thereby ensuring Humphrey's nomination at the Chicago convention in late August. Whether Humphrey's "politics of joy" was enough to keep the Democrats in control of the White House for another term was soon thrown into doubt: the convention's turmoil, along with the violence in the streets, revealed to the country the extent to which the Vietnam War had undermined the Democratic party's former unity and cohesiveness.

Richard Nixon knew that Hubert Humphrey had been badly wounded by the events surrounding the Chicago convention. Yet, his own political resurrection had been one of the remarkable achievements of the sixties. His career appeared to have ended as a result of his decisive defeat in the California governor's race of 1962. But after the Goldwater debacle of 1964, Nixon subsequently positioned himself to move back into the political arena. And in 1968 he was ready once more to become a prime-time player in quest of the Republican presidential nomination. Always a wily candidate, Nixon courted key figures in the South, including Senator Strom Thurmond of South Carolina, to help him secure the nomination, by promising them that if elected he would do his best to halt the advances made by the civil rights movement of the sixties.

Nixon's effort to build conservative bridges to the South was an explicit acknowledgment on his part that as a result of Goldwater's success in 1964 the region had become a major power bloc inside the

Republican party. No longer was the liberal Northeast wing in a position to dictate to the rest of the party, as had been the case in the years when New York governor Thomas Dewey, twice the Republican presidential nominee, could call the shots and get the results he wanted.

During the campaign, Nixon and his running mate, Maryland governor Spiro Agnew, sought to exploit the "social issue" that George Wallace had already advanced to the forefront of national politics even before his third-party bid for the White House had taken final form. Defined as a growing white fear of black street crime, disgust with urban riots, resentment of student rebels, and opposition to perceived special treatment for blacks, it was used by Nixon in a more subtle manner than it was by the surly Alabaman. He made his point by emphasizing the need for tougher law enforcement and a more effective criminal justice system.

Vice-President Hubert Humphrey, meanwhile, was doing his best to pull the Democratic party together. During the campaign he emphasized the traditional economic agenda of the Democratic party, reminding voters of the benefits they had received as a result of the New Deal and post–World War II liberalism. But the economy was not the big issue that year. The Vietnam War and urban riots dominated events in a way that undercut Humphrey's appeal to the memories of the New Deal. Nevertheless, he was helped by a major effort from organized labor, the return of some Eugene McCarthy supporters, and LBJ's October peace initiative. Although Humphrey managed to close the gap between himself and Nixon, he still lost the election by a hair's-breadth. Each received approximately 43 percent of the vote; while George Wallace, carrying the deep South, took nearly 14 percent. More specifically, Nixon won the rim South, including Tennessee, Virginia, and North Carolina, and he nearly swept the West. Humphrey won a number of big states, including New York, Pennsylvania, and Texas. But he could not overcome Nixon's built-in advantage in the West and upper South nor the loss to Wallace of the former Democratic stronghold in the lower South.

Why did Humphrey lose? According to Nixon, it was not Vietnam that defeated him; it was, rather, the demise of the New Deal coalition. Nixon, a shrewd tactician, was on to something very important. As a result of the white backlash, Humphrey had won only 35 percent of the white vote, which surely cost him every state of the old Confederacy save Texas. Moreover, many voters, now more fearful of moral disorder and social instability than their economic future, ignored his traditional appeals for economic justice, made in a period of great prosperity. Having benefited from many past Democratic programs, from Social Security to the Federal Housing Authority, they could afford to focus on other matters, including the continuation of the Vietnam War, street crime, and the unsettling impact of the counterculture. But despite Humphrey's loss, the Democrats retained control of both houses of Congress by substantial margins, at a time when public support for an activist government was still strong.

While President Nixon and Congress prepared their respective working agendas, political scientist Walter Dean Burnham read the 1968 returns as a further confirmation of his argument that the American party system was in a state of long-term partisan decomposition. Many newly independent voters had left the Republican party in the sixties, and millions of Democrats, in both the North and the South, were now decidedly unhappy with the party, viewing it as largely an instrument for black advancement. Burnham thought it unlikely that the current system could or would produce a critical realignment on which a vital democratic politics depended. Worried that a disintegrating party system could not cope with the increasing racial strife and class tensions so characteristic of national life, Burnham saw disaster ahead "if the historically progressive role of the middle class has been played out."

Although Burnham's point about the possible dangers to democracy growing out of the decomposition of the party system is insightful, his comment about the "progressive role" of the middle class merits further discussion. If racial conflicts contributed to the fragmentation of the old Roosevelt coalition, so did deeply rooted cultural antagonisms separating the old white working class from a new meritocratic-minded professional and managerial middle class. The growing prosperity of the fifties and sixties had made it possible for that new class to emerge from the colleges and universities of the country with a cultural and political agenda that was very different from that of the white lower middle class or working class. Representing the "progressive" middle class, this cohort generally opposed the Vietnam War, favored the decriminalization of marijuana, appeared sympathetic to environmental and consumer causes, and supported civil rights for black Americans and greater equality for women. But the sociocultural values it willingly embraced were clearly at odds with the outlook and beliefs of the socially conservative working-class base of the Democratic party, which had been an essential link in the party's chain of successes since the 1930s.

With the seeds of intense cultural conflict now planted inside the Democratic party, there were those in the GOP who looked forward to the harvest ahead. Kevin Phillips, a conservative political analyst, saw the results of 1968 as a steppingstone to larger possibilities. He believed that they vindicated his strategy of pointing the Republican party in the direction of the Sunbelt and away from the hated eastern establishment, controlled by supporters of New York governor Nelson Rockefeller. By stressing traditional cultural and social values, in the face of the countercultural upheaval, as well as opposition to big governmental agendas tied, above all, to race, he thought that a new Republican (conservative) majority could be created. According to his design, Catholic blue-collar voters of the North would join forces with disgruntled white southerners to reconfigure American politics and put conservatives in power.

Phillips had seen the future, and he thought it would work. Much to the eventual benefit and delight of conservatives, many white Americans, including large numbers of traditional Democrats, associated the spread of pornography and rising urban street crime with the Supreme Court's rights-driven legal philosophy and a permissive liberal establishment located in Washington. Consequently, they enlisted in a cultural war over values that began in earnest in the sixties, pitting moral traditionalists and social conservatives against liberal secularists. On one side were those who believed that the changes in the public realm wrought by the practitioners of "legal liberalism" threatened the basis of a proper moral order for America. On the other were members of the secular and cultural left, who strongly favored the ongoing secularization and desegregation of the country's institutions, which had been initiated by the Warren Court and sustained by the Burger Court. Having embraced the "rights revolution," those liberals would soon become the heart and soul of the McGovern movement of the early seventies.

Needless to say, President Nixon was keen to profit from that growing cultural turmoil and racial division, which had already worked so well for him in 1968. In an effort to co-opt Wallace supporters as well as disaffected Democrats, he commissioned Vice-President Agnew to appeal to the Silent Majority, or Middle Americans, via "the politics of positive polarization." Thus, at a time when a majority of Americans were focused on social issues, not the economy, bashing radical liberals as "Sunshine" patriots and attacking apologists for student mayhem and racial upheaval became his number one priority. Nixon spoke out against court-ordered busing, pressed home the need for tighter law enforcement procedures, and nominated conservatives to the Supreme Court. And he also decried the tactics and objectives of the antiwar movement, which, in his opinion, made it more difficult to negotiate a proper "peace with honor" in Vietnam.

While Nixon harped on the "social issue," he also supported the Equal Employment Opportunity Commission's (EEOC) efforts to implement a policy of "preferential treatment for minorities" in employment practices. Having embraced this policy in order to increase strife between blacks and organized labor inside the national Democratic party, he blocked moves in Congress to set aside "racial quotas" his administration had pushed in the construction industry, and he won congressional backing to give the EEOC added authority to advance a strong affirmative action agenda via the mechanism of court-enforced appeals and rulings. After Nixon made these moves, and after the Supreme Court unanimously decided in the 1971 case of Griggs v. Duke Power Co. to support the operating procedures and goals of the EEOC, many white males now had reason to fear that they were going to be victimized by the politics of "reverse discrimination." Ironically, then, when conservatives later launched a massive counterattack against affirmative action programs, it was directed at the legacy of a Republican president who had promoted them for politically motivated reasons.

In the meantime, Nixon offered little resistance to the growing power of the environmental and consumer bloc in Congress. According to business historian David Vogel, that development was tied to an important change in the mood and outlook of an emerging professional and managerial middle class, which was as anti-corporatist in spirit as it was pro-environment and consumerist in ideology. Because this "new class" was politically well connected, especially in various congressional districts around the country, it provided a base of support for a powerful new public interest lobby whose chief spokesman and symbol was Ralph Nader, the leading consumer advocate of the day.

Consequently, in the period from 1969 to 1972, an extraordinary number of bills, reflecting the power of the consumer and environmental movements, passed Congress, including such important measures as the Clean Air Act, the Occupational Safety and Health Act, and the National Environmental Policy Act. The fact that Congress sanctioned such a remarkable expansion of governmental authority over business, which had its roots in the congressional legislation of the mid-sixties, was almost unprecedented; and it indicated that corporate America was poorly prepared to cope with a new regulatory wave then sweeping over Congress. It also indicated that a well-funded and well-organized lobby, relying on a strong grass-roots mobilization and good political connections, could influence the legislative agenda to its advantage. Ironically, the success of the public interest lobby in this instance would provide business at a later stage with a model of how to win friends and influence people at a strategic point in the struggle to roll back the reach of the regulatory state.

Significantly, business did not receive much help from Nixon, who generally went along with Congress's wishes, largely because of his indifference to a business or corporate agenda. And that may explain why he signed into law, on December 30, 1969, the most progressive tax bill ever presented to Congress by a Republican president. He originally proposed to raise the capital gains tax, to abolish John Kennedy's investment tax credit for business, and to provide tax relief for the most marginal and least affluent income earners. The bill, in its final form, not only retained much of what Nixon requested, it lowered the oil depletion allowance as well. Its passage speaks volumes about then-current public attitudes and Nixon's own political priorities during his first term in office.

The American people wanted their environment protected and the health and safety of workers safeguarded. Nixon went along, not because he was a Great Society liberal in disguise, but because he had his own agenda and needs. He sought to preempt the environmental issue and use it for his own purposes, recognizing that Senator Edmund Muskie, a leading spokesman for the environmentalists, would be a likely Democratic challenger in 1972. In addition, by going along with tightened health and safety regulations, he could conceivably appeal to working-class voters in 1972. But apart from these political considerations, he was preoccupied with foreign policy matters, especially Vietnam; they occupied most of his time and reflected his real interests. For him, domestic issues were important when placed in the broader political context of preparing for the 1972 presidential election.

That broader political context also helps to explain why public interest lobbies were able to triumph as they did from 1969 to 1973. As long as the prevailing attitudes among significant blocs of voters, especially among the professional and managerial middle class, were nominally antibusiness and hostile to the rich and to "hippies," that is, as long as there was optimism about the capacity of the economy to produce growth and prosperity, it was possible to undertake those legislative initiatives without fear of jeopardizing the economic well-being of the American people with an intrusive statism.

The sixties, after all, had been a period of remarkable prosperity as the American economy boomed, stimulated by Vietnam spending and the continuing rise in real wages and high corporate profits. It averaged 5 percent growth between 1965 and 1969, and inflation was kept at a reasonably tolerable level. In fact, during the period from 1947 to 1972, the rise in median real income had created more purchasing power than all previous periods combined. The Keynesian welfare state was flourishing to such an extent that in 1969 Daniel P. Moynihan, a former Johnson official now working for Nixon, urged the government to spend generously "in the public interest" in order to avoid fiscal drag.

As a result of the boom of the sixties, Paul Samuelson, a renowned Keynesian economist, was convinced that Nirvana was now in sight. In his view, the business cycle had been conquered because in 1967 America had discovered the equivalent of a perpetual motion machine that could generate a 3.5 percent annual growth rate, perhaps forever. And Herbert Marcuse, a Marxist philosopher, agreed with Samuelson that "abundance" had become the chief characteristic of American capitalism, though he decried this reality on the grounds that it furthered a system of psychological repression, not personal or class liberation.

In actuality, the success of the American system was predicated on a post-1950 arrangement whereby corporate America provided high wages; the federal government stimulated the investment process; and each, in its own way, supported a variety of social programs that enhanced the purchasing power of American workers. As a consequence of this arrangement, determined by the values of social harmony rather than class conflict, corporate profits climbed and purchasing power grew. That was the heart of the liberal welfare state during the years when the United States remained the only hegemonic global power.

Yet the situation was not static, either at home or abroad. By

1971, American global economic power was visibly declining, which was part of a process that had been under way for some time. And though political scientist David Calleo perceptively remarks that this development marked a shift to a more normally pluralist international economic order, the data are striking and revealing. The American share of the world GNP dropped from 40 percent in 1950 to 23 percent in 1970. Its share of world trade stood at 20 percent in 1950; by 1970, it had declined to 11 percent. In the meantime, the United States was being integrated into a global economy to such an extent that imports now pouring into the home market began to compete effectively with American firms in a once exclusive and privileged domain. In addition, inflation was now averaging over 4 percent a year; productivity rates, having peaked in 1966, had dropped significantly; and corporate profits had slipped from 13.7 percent in 1965 to about 8 percent a year during the Nixon years.

This was the context for President Nixon's New Economic Policy, which he announced on August 15, 1971. By seeking to restore a favorable economic position for the United States at home and in world markets, Nixon temporarily slapped a 10 percent surtax on imports; he also took steps to lessen the pressure on the American dollar by devaluing the dollar and declaring that it would no longer be redeemable in gold. Such were the drastic measures he employed to force the West Germans and the Japanese to revaluate their currencies in an upward direction. In addition, he placed price and wage controls on the domestic economy in an attempt to contain inflation and to lower corporate costs. Having gone this far, Nixon seemed to have the economy on his side preparatory to the 1972 election.

Yet, one more move was necessary in order to ensure that the economy was working in Nixon's favor. Arthur Burns, who had been appointed chairman of the Federal Reserve Board by Nixon, remembered well that his old friend had probably lost the 1960 election because of a sluggish economy. Hence, he increased the money supply by 6.1 percent in the 1971–72 period and lowered the discount rate to 4.5 percent until after the election. Nixon also did his part with extra fiscal stimulation that incurred a sizable budget deficit. Thanks to their combined initiatives, a political business cycle was now in place for the purpose of reelecting a newly self-professed Keynesian to a second term.

As the 1972 election approached, the Democrats still faced a serious internal split no matter what Nixon did. Vietnam remained a divisive issue, as it had been in the sixties, when issue-oriented left-liberals refused to support LBJ's war. Now George Meany, the head of the AFL-CIO, and Senator Henry Jackson and his many supporters refused to cooperate with the party's presidential nominee, South Dakota's Senator George McGovern, because they opposed his anti-war position. On the other side, many McGovernites endorsed the political agenda and social policies associated with affirmative action programs, forced busing, and demands for the legalization of marijuana, which threatened the traditional cultural values of the blue-collar Catholic working class and many Wallace supporters in the South. How ironic it was, then, that the major force for cultural change issued from a growing, relatively secure, postindustrial new class, while the main line of opposition to its program and values came from below. The situation was, as pollster Louis Harris described it, "Karl Marx upside down."

McGovern won the nomination because he had been the beneficiary of a number of important primary victories that followed Senator Edmund Muskie's withdrawal from the race earlier in the spring. But McGovern had been seriously wounded by rival Hubert Humphrey in their public debate preceding the California primary. Senator Humphrey, who had returned to the Senate in 1970, vigorously defended the older liberalism against McGovern's program, thereby driving a wedge between himself and McGovern. Although both advocated the use of big government to tackle basic social ills, Humphrey rejected such McGovern-like objectives as income redistribution and a major cut in the military budget.

The Miami convention marked the climax of the New Politics era inside the Democratic party. With McGovern's people in control of the party's machinery, the Illinois delegation, led by Chicago Mayor Richard J. Daley, was forced to leave the convention because it did not conform to the affirmative action requirements mandated by the party, which required the seating of a specific number of blacks, women, and other minorities. It was replaced by one that included the Reverend Jesse Jackson, whose delegation to the convention met those guidelines. Daley's removal constituted a victory of sorts for the McGovern supporters, but as Mike Royko, a Chicago newspaper columnist, remarked, "Anybody who would reform Chicago's Democratic party by dropping the white ethnic would probably begin a diet by shooting himself in the stomach."

And McGovernites did just that. They passed a platform that

went far to support the "rights" of marginalized groups in American society, thereby further inflaming the passions and hostility of many old-line Democrats, who believed that their party had been taken from them by an educated elite for whom a cultural agenda was more important than economic issues and concerns. Would such a serious division over values and beliefs have taken place inside the Democratic party if either Muskie or Humphrey had been the party's nominee? Could it be that the long-term interests of the Democratic party had been sacrificed by McGovern's nomination, which drove many working-class Democrats into the arms of the GOP, thereby helping to create the basis for a conservative triumph in the years to come?

Subsequent to the convention, news was leaked that McGovern's running mate, Senator Thomas Eagleton, had undergone shock therapy. Although McGovern promised to stand by him 1,000 percent, he quickly dumped Eagleton in favor of Sargent Shriver, the former Peace Corps director with Kennedy family connections. Following this fiasco, Richard Nixon had little need to worry. In fact, Nixon's chances of winning had already been substantially enhanced by the misfortune of George Wallace, who had been paralyzed from the waist down following an assassination attempt in Laurel, Maryland, on May 15, the day before he won both the Maryland and Michigan Democratic primaries. With Wallace no longer able to campaign for the 1972 Democratic nomination, he withdrew from the race, leaving millions of his supporters to fall into Nixon's hands in November.

During the campaign, the president presented his basic themes, which were designed to attract southern whites and northern blue-collar workers to his cause. He shrewdly countered McGovern's call for more governmental programs by emphasizing family values, the work ethic, self reliance, and the need for a less intrusive federal government. Yet just before the election, Nixon signed legislation granting cost-of-living allowances to Social Security recipients.

Nixon was not denied what he had long sought; he won forty-nine out of the fifty states, losing only Massachusetts and the District of Columbia. Capturing nearly 61 percent of the popular vote, he almost matched LBJ's percentage of 1964. All in all, it appeared that his goal of creating a new American majority was well within reach. But realignment did not come with the 1972 election. Nixon's triumph was on one level a repudiation of George McGovern by an electorate that viewed the Democrat as an incompetent politician whose extremist messages on social issues and on war and peace were out of touch with mainstream values and beliefs. But Nixon's failure to dislodge a Democratic majority in Congress was an indication that ticket splitting on the national level had become a habit. The Democrats kept their solid majority in the House and picked up two additional seats in the Senate, aided no doubt by Nixon's refusal to campaign for his party on that level.

Nevertheless, this election went far to confirm the accuracy and validity of what Walter Dean Burnham had said earlier about the current state of American politics. From his perspective, the process of partisan decomposition and dealignment was as much in evidence in 1972 as it had been in 1968. The combination of massive ticket splitting and Nixon's failure to integrate a floating mass of discontented voters into a viable Republican majority in Congress suggested that the process of realignment had been thwarted on the grassroots level.

Yet, in one region the American political system had clearly changed, resulting from the irreversible break-up of the New Deal coalition on the level of presidential politics. Inspired by the politics of race and fueled by cultural resentment, a realignment was well under way in the South, precipitated by the Goldwater campaign of 1964 and the efforts of Nixon and Wallace in 1968 and 1972. Many white southerners now believed that the party of their fathers had turned into a vehicle to promote black aspirations across the country. Their resentment of Washington's interventionist social policies (shared by many voters across the country) helped to dissolve old party loyalties, contributing to the growth of an important bloc of independent voters and of many newly enfranchised Republicans everywhere in the South, particularly among members of the suburban middle class and the important business community.

Nixon had pushed hard during the campaign to create a conservative coalition inside the Republican party by bringing ethnic Catholics in the North into an alliance with southern white Protestants. The key to such a fusion had been the "social issue": on the level of ideology and practice, voters across the country who were hostile to the advanced liberal agenda of McGovern Democrats found themselves in agreement. Whether that relationship, which had transformed presidential politics in the South, was strong enough to withstand an economic downturn and the possible return to the class-dominated issues of New Deal days was a question that the 1972 election could not answer.

The day after his reelection, President Nixon informed a reporter that the sixties had been a failure because the government "threw money at problems." That effort had produced, in his words, "a breakdown in frankly what I would call the leadership class of the country." Saying in so many words that the answer to governmental inefficiency was less government, Nixon was seeking to justify attempts to curb the power of the federal bureaucracy and to begin the task of rolling back those many Great Society programs that he had funded fairly generously during his first term. Moving away from his domestic centrist straddle, Nixon was also burying forever his one-time brief commitment to a Family Assistance Program, which he had made at Daniel P. Moynihan's urging for the purpose of providing a guaranteed annual income for America's poorest families.

Nixon's expressed belief that the Great Society had largely wasted the public's money was a staple of conservative antiwelfare ideology, which could be found in many articles published in such journals as *The Public Interest* and *Commentary*. The fact that sophisticated academic analysts supported a point of view that Nixon himself had embraced meant that the intellectual and ideological terrain, which had been dominated for years by a set of liberal beliefs and arguments, would no longer remain uncontested. The rise of academic neoconservatism, coinciding more or less with Nixon's own shift in public policy, was going to have a significant impact on how social issues were perceived and debated by intellectual and policy elites in the future.

Nixon's earlier political flexibility had been shaped by the fact that he could not yet completely repudiate the moderate-liberal wing of his party whose representation in Congress was still a factor that he sometimes had to consider when making policy or appointments. More important, he also had to deal with Democrats whose control of Congress forced him to work with them on a variety of social and economic issues. But once the 1972 election had given him a plebiscitary mandate to roll back the welfare state and to trim the federal bureaucracy, he was determined to have his own way. Hence, in the early days of 1973, he impounded congressionally appropriated funds for social programs whose objectives he opposed. And he all but dared Congress to impeach him if it did not like his stance, before the humbling process of accountability in the context of the Watergate scandal reduced him to the status of Citizen Nixon a year and half later.

Watergate involved a break-in at the headquarters of the Democratic National Committee in June 1972 by people who took their orders from the White House. Ultimately an investigation of this incident revealed that Nixon himself had played the central role in seeking to cover up the fact that individuals connected to his administration were intimately involved in that crime. As a result of this discovery, Nixon not only lost his standing with Congress, where he soon faced impeachment proceedings, but he also lost the respect of the country.

The Watergate affair was, as Senator William Fulbright remarked, akin "to the bursting of a boil," and its effect was to remove Nixon from office. But there were other developments within the general time frame of Watergate that also had important consequences for the future of American politics and society. They included the return of inflation, growing opposition to the proposed Equal Rights Amendment to the Constitution (ERA), and the Supreme Court's *Roe v. Wade* decision in 1973 legalizing abortion.

Inflation reappeared after Nixon removed mandatory price and wage controls in February 1973. But because it was even more virulent than before, the price level quickly jumped to an annual rate of 9.5 percent, months before OPEC increased its price on exported oil. Both Nixon and Arthur Burns had helped to lay the groundwork for that inflationary explosion, even though the OPEC price hike later greatly accelerated it. They had pumped billions into the economy in 1972 via a political business cycle to ensure that full employment would result in time to affect the outcome of the election. Nixon got what he wanted—and now the American people felt the effects, in the form of rocketing price hikes in the sensitive food and housing sectors. The genie of inflation was out of the bottle, and it was destined to have a major impact on national political and economic life in the years to come.

While Nixon was caught in the coils of Watergate, a movement began to block the state-by-state ratification of the Equal Rights Amendment, which would prohibit discrimination on the basis of sex and which had cleared Congress with Nixon's belated endorsement in 1972. The mobilization to derail ERA was led by Phyllis Schlafly, who was blessed with exceptional organizational and public relations skills. By the same token, abortion foes geared up for a political struggle on the state and congressional levels. In the making, then, was a counteragenda to the liberal social programs of the Democratic party and those Supreme Court decisions associated with the "rights revolution." And as a result of that development, which went along with the rise of academic neoconservatism, liberalism was no longer in a position to dominate the political discourse of American life. Instead, this period marked the beginning of a serious and rapid decline in the fortunes of liberalism, which would last for years to come.

Beginning with the New Deal era, an informal liberal establishment, with the power to influence national policy, had functioned as a quasi-official government. Included in its ranks were economists from the Brookings Institution, policy planners at the Ford Foundation, social scientists and law professors from Harvard University and other elite institutions, journalists from the *New York Times* and the *Washington Post*, representatives from organized labor, and powerful public interest law firms in Washington. In a programmatic sense, this establishment generally supported the civil rights movement, endorsed the use of interventionist economics to safeguard the system from another depression, and sought to enlarge the welfare state. And it also provided the intellectual muscle and political base for a containment-oriented foreign policy. But after the disaster of Vietnam and growing opposition to the agenda of big government liberalism, its glory days were at an end, preparing the way at a later stage for a politically mature counter-establishment to define the priorities and goals of the larger national society.

In the meantime, Nixon's days were numbered. On August 9, 1974, he resigned from office and was replaced by Vice-President Gerald Ford, a cautious mainstream Republican who had served for years as the minority leader in the House of Representatives. In retrospect, Nixon can be seen as a transitional president who temporarily came to terms with the Great Society while making plans to undercut it. He also helped to push the roots of presidential Republicanism well below the topsoil of the Sunbelt, thereby altering the political configuration of power within both his party and the country. Yet in 1974, as a result of Watergate and a stagflation-ridden economy, the Republican party stood at 23 percent in the opinion polls, the lowest ever recorded. Nevertheless, more Americans were now willing to identify themselves as conservatives rather than liberals, which was just the reverse of the situation in the mid-sixties. Did this mean, then, that a majority of voters were ideologically and programmatically yearning for a Roosevelt of the Right? Only time and circumstances could answer that question.

The Conservative Upsurge, 1974–1976

As a result of Watergate, Richard Nixon's political fate was sealed by early 1974. Nevertheless, a number of leading conservatives, including California governor Ronald Reagan, stayed with him to the end. But many on the right, along with William Buckley, editor of the *National Review*, felt betrayed by Nixon, seeing him as someone whose fall had deprived conservatives of a chance to implement their program and to realign the national political parties in their favor. Others such as Kevin Phillips saw Watergate as an attempt by liberals to nullify the results of the 1972 election.

As conservatives mulled over their political prospects, most Americans focused on the dramatic jump in the rates of inflation and unemployment. As mentioned earlier, inflation again took hold in early 1973 because Nixon lifted price and wage controls at a time when there was already an excess supply of money, and because massive borrowing by corporations and consumers alike fueled a price surge that OPEC and a worldwide food shortage greatly stimulated as well.

More specifically, a dramatic growth in corporate debt—leading to a major jump in short-term loans to corporations in need of a financial transfusion—contributed to the making of an inflationary environment. In 1974, that borrowing and spending pattern meant that corporate debt was up 152.8 percent in relation to the GNP while the government's share declined to 46 percent. Yet when such members of the financial establishment as Federal Reserve Board Chairman Arthur Burns and Albert Sommers of the Conference Board argued that governmental spending, along with "a tide of social demands," was responsible for inflation, they put the onus for it on the backs of the poorest and weakest members of American society. Their argument, building on Nixon's earlier contention that the government had thrown money at problems, was part of the growing conservative attack directed at the Keynesian welfare state, which would grow in intensity as the decade progressed.

In reality, governmental spending in the welfare sector largely benefited the middle class, not the poor, since Social Security and Medicare received the bulk of governmental funds appropriated for social programs. Nevertheless, the widespread feeling that the government was giving untold billions to impoverished black Americans infuriated lower-middle-class and working-class whites, who had to cope with an economy beset by a simultaneous inflationary surge and recession.

According to economist Douglas Hibbs, inflation was generally "neutral" with respect to income distribution. At best, it may have even marginally improved the position of the bottom 20 percent of income earners. On the other hand, that continuing upward movement of prices undermined the economic interests of bond holders and cut into the post-tax profits of some corporations. But whether one was helped or hurt by moderate inflation, few disagreed with President Gerald Ford when he declared that unemployment affected only 8 percent of the populace but that inflation touched everyone.

If inflation was a troublesome fact of life for most people, the harsh reality of unemployment also affected many Americans. During the period 1974–75, it reached 9 percent, the highest figure since the 1930s. As in the case of inflation, the Federal Reserve Board was partly to blame for that situation. It reduced the money supply and raised interest rates, just as OPEC price hikes were beginning to take their toll at the gas pumps across the country. Consequently, industrial production fell by 15 percent and unemployment jumped accordingly; but inflation did not decline by very much. In short, the Phillips Curve, which postulated that higher unemployment would work to reduce inflation, was now undercut by the new economic reality of stagflation. That is, a higher rate of unemployment, coupled with continuing and persistent inflation, clearly signaled that the era of stable and steady economic growth and low inflation had ended. Significantly, too, the Keynesian prescription for continuing progress, which required social investments from both industry and government, had suddenly become problematic.

The serious erosion of productivity in this same period further complicated the economic picture. By 1975, productivity had declined to an average annual rate of 1 percent, well below the 3.2 percent of the sixties. Why that happened is hard to explain. Economist Edward Denison, an informed student of the subject, called it a "mystery," suggesting, in effect, that a multiplicity of factors were at work, including a changing work force tied to a rapid growth of the service sector. Whatever the exact reasons for the decline, the bottom line was that fewer economic resources would be available for either wage hikes or larger corporate profits. And now corporate America began to view both organized labor and the regulatory arm of the federal government as the culprits most responsible for increasing its labor costs in a new era of falling after-tax profit margins and fierce international competition.

While the forces of stagflation took hold, causing concern and anxiety on all levels of American society, the United States was, at the same time, facing defeat in Vietnam. But Vietnam itself played little or no role in shaping the outcome of the 1974 congressional election. Watergate and a sour economy drove voters to reject a Republican party that was seen as the party of misrule and incompetence. Hence, the Democrats picked up forty-nine seats in the House and added five more in the Senate, making it appear as if they had the political muscle to deal effectively with anything President Ford threw their way. But despite its massive victory in 1974, the Democratic party was not what it once had been. The fall-off in support from blue-collar voters in the North and white southerners, which began in the fifties, was not entirely reversed even though the Democrats were able to return at least to their 1968 voting levels. In short, despite Watergate, the party's New Deal base continued to contract.

Watergate, contends journalist Thomas Edsall, was a pyrrhic victory for the Democrats, coming at a time when they were still sorely in need of political retrenchment. The party had not yet recovered from the political wounds resulting from the cultural and foreign policy wars of the late sixties and early seventies. Six years after the debacle of Chicago, issues such as forced busing and affirmative action programs continued to split various racial and ethnic constituencies inside the party in ways that would prove hard to repair.

As exemplified in the case of the Boston busing controversy of 1974–75, it was a largely ethnic blue-collar class that had to bear the burden of the court-ordered integration of a public school system very much in a state of administrative and physical decay and financial collapse. As if this terrible racial and ethnic turf war was not enough to weaken the liberal wing of the Democratic party, black street crime and white fears were also on the ascendant in many cities across the country. Consequently, blue-collar hostility to blacks and to feminist causes was a growing Democratic party dilemma for which there was no easy answer or quick political fix. Opposed to paying higher taxes for unworkable welfare programs, and frustrated by affirmative action programs that in some cases denied them promotions or vocational opportunities, lower-middle-class and working-class white Americans were full of anxiety and fear about the future. Given their economic and psychological plight, many of them responded favorably to Richard Nixon's and George Wallace's argument that the enemy was big government and its social programs designed to aid the black poor and/or a marginally mobile black lower middle class.

And while that conflict intensified along the racial and ethnic fault lines of an older urban America, the black-Jewish alliance—a keystone of the northern Democratic party—was also disintegrating, as a result of basic disagreements about the implementation of affirmative action programs, the Israeli-Palestinian conflict, and black rejection of a perceived history of Jewish paternalism. Ironically, though, as these one-time close working partners began to go separate ways down the tangled path of liberal pluralism, they both remained more steadfastly loyal to the programmatic liberalism of the Democratic party than did any other voting bloc.

Meanwhile, the Republicans continued to make progress in the South. The process of realignment proceeded along lines favorable to the GOP, as a growing middle class and business elites sought to protect and expand an already attractive business environment. At the same time, many of these same Republicans were also in the forefront of a fast-developing conservative movement inside the national party. But whether they could win national power with a conservative agenda, which included lower taxes and opposition to welfare programs and governmental deregulation, was another question. As long as a majority of Americans continued to believe that the Democrats could be better trusted to manage the economy and to produce prosperity than the Republicans, conservatives would still lack the one key issue they needed to realign national politics in their favor.

Helped by the economic downturn and Watergate, congressional Democrats, after 1974, pushed hard to enact a public interest and labor agenda. And they were in a good position to do so, because the country was deeply suspicious of big business as a result of recent revelations that some corporations had been associated with illegal contributions to Nixon's reelection committee. That development presented corporate America with a serious legislative problem. In fact, Bryce Harlow, a sophisticated corporate lobbyist, well understood that as a result of the 1974 election business was faced with a threat "of being rolled up and put in the trash."

Harlow's fears were not exaggerated: Congress soon extended the life of the 1970 Clean Air Act without crippling amendments, and it augmented the powers of the Federal Trade Commission to regulate business. In addition, organized labor, which had been relatively quiet during the earlier activist period of Ralph Nader's public interest lobby, again flexed its muscle, thereby suggesting that business was now facing a two-front assault on its proposals to deal with regulatory matters as well as labor-management relations.

Labor's return to the fray was an important development, because over the years going back to the Roosevelt era—it had been a major force for promoting a liberal policy agenda inside the Democratic party. But ever since the mid-fifties, there had been a slow, steady decline in union membership. Moreover, the union movement itself had lost much of its passion for social reform, to such an extent that the AFL-CIO leadership, excepting people like Walter Reuther, often sat on the sidelines during the great civil rights struggles of the sixties. Also, organized labor generally supported the American intervention in Vietnam down to 1973, producing a major ideological rift between those who identified with the older liberalism of the New Deal and many new-class McGovernites. In addition, those two groups found it hard to work together because of their basic differences over cultural values and class interests. That is, labor cared little for the affirmative action programs or the social concerns of many "life-style liberals": conversely, its economic agenda bored many upper-middle-class McGovernites, who identified more with ghetto blacks than with the needs and concerns of the white working class. Nevertheless, most mainstream Democrats understood that their party's past political success, as well as their current and future hopes, still greatly depended upon labor's financial resources and considerable mobilizing skills.

Congressional Democrats in the 94th Congress were receptive to labor's agenda, and they worked hard to pass the Humphrey-Hawkins full employment bill. As the most important piece of social legislation considered by that particular Congress, it authorized the federal government to provide jobs in the public sector for people needing and wanting work by lowering the unemployment rate to 3 percent, well below the current figure of 8 percent of the 1975–76 period. But, as it turned out, the struggle to enact this legislation, although it brought together many different groups to work for its passage, was the last hurrah for the old liberalism.

Marking the return to the old days of coalitional politics, the Congressional Black Caucus, organized labor, public interest lobbies, and environmentalists joined together to work for the passage of a bill whose roots went back to the New Deal. Although the bill's supporters had the votes to clear Congress, their margin of success was not great enough to overcome a projected Ford veto. Consequently, the congressional leadership delayed final floor action on this legislation until a new Congress and, presumably, a new Democratic president could ensure its success in 1977.

While Ford's vetoes stalled that labor-public interest coalition, there were also other developments signifying the emergence of countervailing forces. A corporate backlash against regulation was under way, resulting from action taken by overzealous administrators from the Occupational Safety and Health Administration (OSHA), who, among other things, dictated the size of toilet seats. Their demands fueled outrage among businessmen, who contended that stringent governmental regulations had to cost them profits and productivity gains. In practice, many businessmen had sought to comply with environmental and safety requirements. In 1974, for example, they invested $7.4 billion in air and water controls and over $3 billion in safety equipment, which amounted to 10.8 percent of all capital spending for that year alone. With business pressure now very much on the increase, Congress responded by ordering OSHA to be less protective of some workers. It was a portent of things to come.

Ford, a more corporate-minded Republican than Richard Nixon, vetoed much of the Democratic social and economic legislation. And his program to fight inflation was cut from the same corporate cloth. Symbolized by the acronym WIN (Whip Inflation Now), Ford's program committed his administration to lowering the inflation rate by pursuing a deliberate policy of fiscal restraint and voluntary cooperation among various interest groups. Even in 1976, when it was in his interest to pursue a more stimulative fiscal policy, Ford rejected a "short-term view" and held back. Hence, he refused to spend money in his own budget, which not only contributed to a slowing down of the economy but increased unemployment just before the election.

While President Ford confronted a sluggish economy, Treasury Secretary William Simon argued that a massive capital shortage, amounting to a projected $2.5 trillion over the next ten years, would result from governmental spending policies. Governmental deficits, he claimed, were "crowding out" private firms from the credit markets. To spur productivity via increased investment, Simon urged that the federal government reduce its support of social programs and cut taxes. But Simon's contention notwithstanding, there was ample liquidity available for investment. Not only were corporations able to borrow $100 billion from 1975 to 1980, but from 1970 to 1983 American banks poured $352 billion into the Third World. Yet it did not matter very much that Simon's figures and fears were greatly exaggerated; as a result of a massive business mobilization to come, his argument that the country was facing a serious capital shortage would soon resonate throughout the halls of Congress, thereby justifying in the minds of many politicians the need to reduce the taxes on the corporations and the rich alike.

Despite the Ford administration's embrace of a business agenda, its policies still failed to placate many conservatives on Gerald Ford's right. Led by such New Right stalwarts as Howard Phillips and Paul Weyrich, they remained adamantly opposed to Ford for having selected Nelson Rockefeller as his vice-president; they denounced the president because he did not speak out against a liberal social agenda that included support for abortion and the ERA; and they were unforgiving because he seemed willing to cut an arms deal with Moscow. By the time Ford made plans to run for the GOP nomination in 1976, he had to confront not only the Democrats but a massive bloc of discontented voters inside and outside of his own party, who were looking for a white knight to lead their charge against an allegedly bankrupt Republican presidency.

Conservative intellectuals such as William Rusher, publisher of the *National Review*, and Richard Viguerie, a New Right activist, were in the forefront of that movement to find a challenger to Ford. They even went so far as to consider forming a third party in order to run George Wallace and Ronald Reagan, the recently retired governor of California, against him. That some conservatives were prepared to oppose Ford spoke volumes about their alienation from the GOP and the strength of their convictions about those social issues that mattered the most to them.

Viguerie was a key figure in any movement to form such a third party. A former executive secretary of the Young Americans for Freedom who had developed his promotional skills in the Goldwater campaign of 1964, he later worked with George Wallace, helping him to retire his campaign debts for 1972. From Wallace he received millions of new names to bank for future references and solicitations. In short, Viguerie was ahead of everyone else on the right, exploiting the new computer technology for the purpose of compiling a formidable list of campaign supporters and contributors, which he could later draw upon for campaign purposes.

Even William Buckley, editor of the *National Review*, at first sympathized with a third party strategy until Reagan announced in 1975 that he would seek the Republican presidential nomination. Worried about Wallace's populism, Buckley decided to work inside the Republican party for Reagan, endorsing a third party option only if Reagan himself, were he denied the GOP nomination, led such a movement.

As an election year approached, conservatives appeared to differ among themselves as to what strategy would best serve their common goal of finding someone to carry their banner in 1976. And those differences made it appear as if a serious ideological rift had developed inside the conservative movement between the supporters of the New Right and the Old Right. According to Kevin Phillips, the New Right, which had something of a pro-Wallace flavor, was oriented to a populist agenda that "puts principal emphasis on domestic social issues—on public anger over busing, welfare spending, environmental extremism, soft criminology, media bias and power, warped education, twisted textbooks, racial quotas, various guidelines, and an ever-expanding bureaucracy." The Old Right, claimed Phillips, was an elitist, "high church religion," opposed to mass culture and politics and mostly interested in "national security, free market economics . . . and U.S.-Soviet detente." Having said that much, he, too, endorsed a Reagan-Wallace ticket for 1976.

The dichotomy that Phillips imposed on the conservative movement bears closer examination. Phillips and others who shared his point of view argued that a conservative populism was at the heart of the New Right, distinguishing it from the older conservatism of the fifties and sixties. In actuality, though, those differences separating the Old and the New Right were really at bottom tactical and not always so markedly ideological. As Viguerie himself admitted, "There is not a great deal that is new about the New Right. Our views, our philosophy, our beliefs, are not that different, if at all, from the Old Right. It is our emphasis that is different at times."

Viguerie's comment highlights an important point, developed well by sociologist Jerome Himmelstein, that continuity in outlook, program, goals, and even personalities characterized both the New and the Old Right, whose common roots went back to the fifties and early sixties. The seventies, he argues, did not represent a break with the past. Rather, it was a period when some conservatives, in an attempt to cope with an altered economic and social environment, not only updated the message and perspective of an earlier period but used new tactics and organizational methods to develop a mass base for their causes.

That older conservatism, from which the New Right sprang, was tied to a philosophy of limited government and moral traditionalism at home and the rollback of communism abroad. And in the fifties and sixties, no one was more important in disseminating that perspective than William Buckley. Almost single-handedly, he had been responsible for bringing together the various elements on the Right, including free-market conservatives and militant anticommunists, to write for the *National Review*. A feisty, often nasty, but generally well-edited weekly, it won ideological converts to a variety of right-wing causes, especially on conservative college campuses, at a time when the intellectual terrain was very much dominated by an establishment liberalism that was beginning to identify with the civil rights movement of Martin Luther King.

Afterwards, conservatives of the Buckley persuasion gained a certain leverage and legitimacy inside the American political system via Barry Goldwater's triumph at the Republican convention in 1964; they built on that experience and success by creating a cadre of right-wing professionals, whose good campus and corporate connections helped them gain further respectability. Meanwhile, they worked hard to mobilize support for their program, which also included opposition to the ERA, forced busing, and abortion.

As a result of changes in the rules and regulations governing the selection of delegates to the Republican National Convention, those conservatives were given an opportunity to make further headway inside the Republican party. Once party officials realized that the many Democratic primaries were attracting close media attention, they sought to obtain the same benefits for their candidates. Hence, they opened their system to accommodate the television camera by making it easier for candidates to find delegate support via the primary route. The impact of that shift was immediate and dramatic. In 1972, 53 percent of the delegates to the Republican National Convention emerged from presidential primaries; by 1976, that figure jumped to 68 percent, which helped to push the GOP farther and faster to the right, since so many more party activists involved in the primary process were now conservatives.

As television was fast becoming the arbiter of the political process, so too was the importance of money in the promotion of candidates and causes. Corporate America was ready to take advantage of new laws governing campaign financing to reach voters, or potential voters, who might support their candidates. Ironically, a 1974 amendment to the 1971 Federal Election Campaign Act, which sought to reform the process by which contributions were made to individual candidates, was a key development in promoting a future Republican revival. Congress, seeking to avoid a repetition of the financial scandal involving the 1972 Nixon reelection committee, tried to remedy that situation by setting a $1,000 limit on how much an individual could contribute to a given candidate, and it placed a $5,000 limit on direct contributions from political action committees. But after the Supreme Court ruled in *Buckley v. Valeo* (1976) that corporations could solicit funds from their employees for political purposes, PACs became an ever more important weapon in the hands of skilled political entrepreneurs opposing the legislative bent of a liberal-minded Congress.

At a time when many corporations started to flex their political muscles, Ronald Reagan prepared to retire as governor of California in 1974. Blessed with acute good luck and a sense of timing, which did much to advance his political career, he had thought of running against incumbent senator Alan Cranston, but then decided against it. As it turned out, Reagan had made the right move, for the backlash from Watergate had led to a Democratic landslide, which probably would have resulted not only in his defeat that year but the scuttling of those plans he had long since made to run for the White House. In addition, Reagan benefited enormously from George Wallace's misfortune. A victim of an attempted assassination attempt in 1972, Wallace was no longer physically able to mount the kind of campaign charge that had earlier made him a much admired and hated figure across the country. Consequently, a part of the Wallace constituency, and some of his financial support, moved elsewhere in 1975, in search of other, more promising candidates and attractive political opportunities. Although Kevin Phillips and Richard Viguerie looked favorably at former Treasury Secretary John Connally, whose charisma and pugnacity appealed to them, he refused to be drawn into the political game, leaving Reagan with a clear field on which to make his moves. He soon emerged as the candidate of choice among most conservatives who hoped to deny Gerald Ford the Republican nomination in 1976.

When Reagan formally announced in November 1975 that he would seek the Republican presidential nomination, he was aware that millions of Republicans were dissatisfied with Ford and embarrassed by Nixon, and that they were looking for a change in direction and leadership. Much to their delight, Reagan had the political credentials to challenge an incumbent president who had been a long-time mainstream Republican loyalist. He had twice been elected governor of California, the state with the most electoral votes; he had telegenic appeal and more than enough funding to undertake a national campaign; and he was the logical spokesman of the growing conservative movement inside the Republican party, at a time of growing dissatisfaction with the status quo.

Reagan's message was clear and to the point: the enemy was the Washington establishment. As he put it in his prepared remarks announcing his candidacy: "Our nation's capital has become the seat of a buddy system that functions for its own benefit—increasingly insensitive to the needs of the American worker who supports it with his taxes. Today it is difficult to find leaders who are independent of the forces that have brought us our problems—the Congress, the bureaucracy, the lobbyists, big business, and big labor." Interestingly, Reagan lumped "big business" together with "big labor," which was a shrewd and revealing juxtaposition, demonstrating that he and his advisers were surely aware that both were now held in low esteem by an overwhelming majority of Americans. It also suggested that he was no spokesman for an older corporate capitalism located in the Midwest or the Northeast. A Sunbelt politician par excellence, Reagan admired successful entrepreneurs from the South and West, who were not dependent upon financial support from the despised Eastern establishment. Over the years a number of these self-made men had become members of his famous "Kitchen Cabinet," including Holmes Tuttle, whose money was made in the retail end of the auto business; Justin Dart, a successful Tupperware promoter; and Charles Wick, who had become independently wealthy as a result of his investments in agribusiness and real estate. They were united by a common detestation of organized labor and the welfare state, as well as a shared belief that Ronald Reagan would make a great president.

When Reagan served as governor of California, he was not quite as hard-line a right-winger as were many of his ideologically minded friends and supporters. For example, his administration substantially increased the state budget that allowed him to spend significant sums in all areas of public education. In addition, he used his power to advance the state's regulatory function. As journalist Alan Crawford points out, he "sponsored . . . one of the toughest water pollution control laws in the United States and stepped up state control over auto repair, home insurance, real estate, retail business, doctors, and dentists. He increased inheritance taxes, provided tax credits for renters, reduced the oil depletion allowance, and stiffened the capital gains tax." In short, Reagan's actual record in California did not quite match the rhetoric that he took with him into the 1976 New Hampshire primary.

Even though he had never won an election outside of his congressional district in western Michigan, President Ford managed to defeat Reagan in New Hampshire by a mere thirteen hundred votes. Admittedly, Reagan ran a poor campaign, refusing to attack Ford as he would soon do in upcoming primaries. Later, while Ford won primary battles in the Northeast and Midwest, Reagan mounted a fierce counterattack elsewhere, especially in the South and the West, by focusing on Ford's foreign policy record. He denounced the policy of detente as a failure and condemned efforts to make an agreement with Panama over the future control of the Panama Canal. As a result of a series of impressive primary victories in the Sunbelt, Reagan closed the gap between himself and the president, heading into the convention with the race in a virtual dead heat.

Aware of the magnitude of Reagan's challenge, Ford had earlier sought to protect his flank by announcing that Vice-President Nelson Rockefeller would not be his running mate in 1976. But the dumping of Rockefeller made little difference to Reagan's supporters. The Ford administration was the symbol of everything they despised: its huge budgetary deficits, its refusal to roll back the welfare state, and its policy of detente reminded them they were part of a larger move-ment to change not just the face of the Republican party but the poli-cies of the federal government as well.

But to the surprise and consternation of Reagan's supporters, Reagan announced in advance of the roll call of the states that mod-erately liberal senator Richard Schweiker of Pennsylvania would be his running mate in the event he won the nomination. Although Schweiker had close working ties with organized labor, he supported the New Right's social agenda, which included opposition to busing and abortion. Despite his strong and consistent stand on those partic-ular issues, Schweiker was still unacceptable to such a hard-line right-wing ideologue as North Carolina's senator Jesse Helms and others like him, who feared that Reagan had betrayed the conserva-tive movement at the last moment.

Unfortunately for Reagan, that shrewd move, taken to broaden his appeal, failed to attract the few delegates he needed to go over the top. Hence, Ford won a very narrow first ballot victory, allowing him to select Kansas's senator Robert Dole as his running mate. On the other hand, though Reagan lost the fight for the nomination, the strength of the movement he led was such that the Republican party endorsed a platform at its Kansas City convention that was far closer to his position than would have been conceivable four years earlier. Having little say in the matter, Ford was forced to accept a platform that was not only critical of detente and possible "secret agreements" with Panama but included conservative positions on busing, abor-tion, and prayer in the public schools. Yet in his acceptance speech, Ford sought to reach beyond the convention by appealing to the country's taxpayers and its law-abiding citizens, including many who were not Republican, "to make . . . my mission possible." Convinced that he had a chance to win, the president declared that "this year the issues are on our side."

The Democrats emphatically disagreed with Ford, believing that his pardon of Richard Nixon and failure to overcome the effects of stagflation would soon lead them back to the White House. But the road they planned to travel was full of potholes and rough spots, suf-ficient in size and number to prevent an easy return to executive power. Their many internal difficulties were compounded by the fact that heading into 1976 they had no candidate in sight who possessed

the personal appeal and/or could deliver the partisan message necessary to mobilize blocs of often antagonistic voters and competing interest groups into a viable political coalition.

Still, there were a number of eager Democratic candidates lined
up to compete for the privilege of running against the Republican
record of Nixon and Ford. And each one represented a splinter or
fraction of a Democratic party that was now a very pale imitation of
Franklin Roosevelt's New Deal coalition. Arizona congressman Morris Udall spoke for many college-educated liberals and some traditional Democrats; Washington's senator Henry Jackson represented
the cold war perspective and domestic political interests of organized
labor; George Wallace articulated the various cultural and racial
grievances of working-class white southerners and northerners alike;
and former Georgia governor Jimmy Carter, with a foot in every
camp and a face for every constituency, wanted the South to send the
American people a president, not just a message.

Carter brilliantly exploited the opportunity that the primary system gave to an outsider like himself to deliver knockout blows to his
opponents. He ruined Wallace's bid for a comeback with a victory in
the Florida primary; he pushed Jackson out of the race with a win in
Pennsylvania; and his narrow victories over Udall in Wisconsin and
Michigan sealed the congressman's fate. But Carter had not yet won
a clear path to the nomination. In fact, stiff competition was still to
come from California governor Jerry Brown and Idaho senator Frank
Church, who, in spite of their late start, won a series of impressive
victories across the country, which suggested that Carter's support
was not very deep or necessarily widespread. But Carter's political
life was saved by his victory in the Ohio Democratic primary, which
not only won him the endorsement of Chicago mayor Richard Daley
but the nomination as well.

Of the various Democratic challengers who stepped forward that
year, none was more interesting than Governor Jerry Brown. Having
succeeded Ronald Reagan as governor, Brown declared that governmental spending was responsible for producing inflation. He also argued that government did not have solutions for all the social ills
plaguing American society. Brown's remarks, coming from someone
with his liberal credentials, served to highlight an important new development inside the Democratic party: he had given expression to a
point of view that other Democrats, including senators Paul Tsongas

and Gary Hart, would later develop and seek to refine. A neoliberal, Brown had counterposed the ideology of limits to the politics of growth.

Much to Brown's chagrin, it was Carter, not Brown, who went to New York to receive the party's nomination. That convention also drafted a liberal platform and confirmed Minnesota senator Walter Mondale, a longtime protege of Hubert Humphrey, as Carter's running mate. In the meantime, Carter worked hard to reconcile the various elements of the party. His approach seemed to work, for he was endorsed by George Wallace and embraced by Martin Luther King, Sr. And most party liberals went along with him in the name of party unity. Leaving the convention with a solid lead in the polls, Carter appeared to be a certain winner in November.

After the Republican convention nominated Gerald Ford, the campaign began in earnest. And by the time it was over, television debates and all, Tom Wicker, a longtime commentator on American politics, remarked that both nominees had spent their time doing nothing more than making "calculated appeals and empty promises." Since neither candidate discussed very much in the way of substance, the outcome of the election hinged on which side could best mobilize its base after those "appeals and promises" had been made. Fortunately for Carter, whose wide lead over Ford had just about disappeared as election day approached, the economic issue provided him with the one issue that he could promote as a good Democrat without fear of alienating any of the otherwise divided elements inside his own party. By holding Ford responsible for the country's persistent inflation and high unemployment, which were worrisome problems for most voters, Carter had succeeded in keeping Ford on the defensive. In addition, Carter probably benefited from Ford's comment, made during one of their televised debates, that Eastern Europe was free of Soviet domination.

Although Carter won only twenty-three states (including ten out of eleven from the South) to Ford's twenty-seven, he obtained a narrow victory in the electoral college, while receiving about 50.1 percent of the popular vote. Carter triumphed because his opposition to forced busing and abortion and his support for populist economics brought back to the party some key voters lost to Nixon in 1972. Consequently, he won the votes of a significant number of southern whites, received support from northern white Protestants, and, at the same time, scored heavily with black voters in both the North and the South. In addition, he received considerable help from the ranks of organized labor.

Yet Carter had not pieced together, in any dynamic way, the old elements of the New Deal coalition. Southern whites gave him, a native son, only 46 percent of their votes, not the usual 70 percent Democratic presidential candidates had once received as a matter of course in Dixie; and the Catholic vote, a key component of the old New Deal coalition, had dropped to 53 percent. In fact, Carter's victory was so razor-thin that a shift in a few thousand votes away from him to Ford in several states, including Ohio, would have sent the incumbent back to the White House. Most revealing, Carter's personal appeal was so lacking that he ran behind 272 of the 292 successful Democrats who were elected to the House of Representatives.

Even though the election returns demonstrate that party affiliation was an important factor in Carter's win, there was still a high degree of ticket splitting that year: a striking 37 percent of voters declared that they were independent of party loyalties and strong partisan commitments. Furthermore, only 54.4 percent of eligible voters went to the polls in 1976, signifying a further drop in interest below that of 1972, which probably meant that Democrats were not attracting as many of their core constituents to the voting booths as they had in the sixties.

Of related interest, then, is the point raised by journalist Thomas Edsall. He noted that many in the freshman class of Democrats who were elected to the House of Representatives in 1976 represented middle-class suburban districts, which had often been Republican in the past. Whether these Democrats would represent the political and economic interests of their own constituents, at the expense of the liberal-labor coalition, would soon be answered in the changing political alignments of the newly elected Democratic 95th Congress.

Although the Democrats were delighted with the election results, conservative Republicans, too, had good reason to be heartened by those same returns. Gerald Ford's defeat meant that control of the Republican party was now up for grabs; and conservatives, alert to this reality, were ready to go to work. Ronald Reagan, eager to do his part, said the day after the 1976 election that the time had come "to use the Republican platform to reach a new majority . . . for the G.O.P."

Jimmy Carter and the Crisis of Liberalism

Jimmy Carter prevailed in 1976 because he won support from both the public interest wing and the labor wing of the Democratic party. During the campaign, he made specific promises to those key interest groups, which indicated his desire to work with them in order to advance their respective agendas. Carter pledged to the public interest group that he would safeguard the environment and promote the cause of a Nader-oriented consumerism. To labor, he made a commitment to work on behalf of common situs and labor reform legislation, as well as the Humphrey-Hawkins Bill.

Although Carter had embraced certain programmatic objectives during that election year, his ideological orientation ran counter to the mainstream thinking of his party. As a moderate southern Democrat, he talked about producing a balanced budget by the end of his four years as president, which meant that his approach to fiscal policy was largely rooted in a managerial, cost-efficient approach to social problems. Moreover, his definitions of what were acceptable rates of inflation and unemployment were similar to those of Gerald Ford, who had been overwhelmingly supported by the business community during the 1976 election.

Carter himself was eager to placate business. Therefore, he appointed Bert Lance, a small-town Georgia banker of conservative views, as his budget chief, and Charles Schultze, a market-oriented Brookings Institution economist, as head of the Council of Economic Advisers. As a further sop to business, Carter quickly dropped any campaign commitment to wage and price controls, hoping to achieve economic growth through fiscal policies that would avoid fueling more inflation.

Like all presidents, Carter understood the need to cooperate as fully as possible with men of corporate power, who held such a privileged position inside the American system of regulated capitalism. At the same time, he was heir to the legacy of liberalism, which had been the ideological and programmatic touchstone of the Democratic party since Franklin Roosevelt's New Deal. A key characteristic of that liberalism was a commitment to interventionist economics and politics, which had made possible the creation and enlargement of the American welfare state. Yet when compared to its European counterparts in either West Germany or Sweden, the American welfare state appeared impoverished, providing only minimal benefits to the working poor or the unemployed. The major share of governmental payouts went to such middle-class programs as Social Security or Medicare, which the Democratic party had proudly legislated over time in the name of social decency and for reasons of good politics.

A key to the preservation or extension of that system of welfare capitalism was a viable American labor movement, which at its best sought to protect the populace from the social ravages of a market system. By the mid-seventies, however, that movement was in deep trouble, precisely at a time when it faced an extraordinary challenge to its position resulting from the globalization of American capitalism and a changing political situation in both Congress and the country.

Even before domestic and international events converged in the mid- and late seventies to erode labor's base inside the Democratic party, the labor movement had been in a state of slow decline. Since the fifties, it had failed to attract new members to compensate sufficiently for the fact that the percentage of workers in unions continued to drop when compared with the growing numbers of unaffiliated workers throughout the country. Despite that slide, which saw labor's percentage of the work force fall from 26 percent to 21 percent in the seventies, George Meany, the president of the AFL-CIO, had stood pat, unable or unwilling to engage in the kinds of struggles that might have broadened the base of his organization at a critical time in its history. What he and other union bureaucrats desired, above all, was access to the White House and to key figures on Capitol Hill, which allowed them to play the game of interest group politics in a manner befitting the elite of the union movement. Meanwhile, labor's rank and file had been benefiting from the great prosperity of the sixties and early seventies; their wages were good, and their purchasing power had kept pace with or exceeded the cost of living. But by the mid-seventies, the good times that they had experienced in the glory years of capitalist growth had largely come to an end.

Not only had stagflation become a way a life for many American workers, unionized or not, but there were other forces at work that affected their economic prospects, as well as the political future of both the labor movement and the Democratic party. Among the most important were the continuing globalization of the American economy and the further decline in productivity at home. As Michael Harrington observed, the seventies marked a period of rapid maturing in most capitalist economies, including Singapore, Japan, South Korea, and Taiwan. In that context, it was necessary for firms located in these countries to find new export markets in order to keep their profit levels from falling. Key American industries such as autos, steel, and electronics soon found themselves facing a tidal wave of quality imports from abroad. Now challenged by world-class competition, they began to move their plants in the direction of either the Sunbelt or the Third World in search of cheap sources of labor to reduce their operating costs.

Statistics revealed much about the economic changes that were taking place at home and overseas, which would soon have a major impact on the national politics of the day. For example, the trade deficit, which stood at $9.5 billion in 1976, expanded to $31.1 billion in 1977 and jumped again in 1978 to over $34 billion. More specifically, from 1975 to 1977 the amount of imported steel increased from 13.5 percent to 17.8 percent of domestic consumption; and foreign auto producers, who had captured about 8 percent of the U.S. home market in 1970, now controlled nearly 22 percent by 1979. In 1970, 8.3 percent of the GNP was tied to exports and imports; by 1980, that figure had jumped to 17.4 percent, indicating the growing extent of America's economic integration into the larger international system.

As these various figures reveal, something profound and important was happening to the country's industrial base, reflecting an underlying crisis that was perhaps best captured by the persistent decline in productivity. In the period from 1973 to 1979, productivity averaged 0.80 percent as compared to 2.44 percent during the years of great prosperity, 1950 to 1973. That decline was abetted by the emergence of a dynamic service sector, represented by Burger King and

McDonald's, which began to employ millions of nonunionized workers at wage rates far below those paid out by the mass production industries. According to economist Lester Thurow, service sector productivity equaled only 61 percent of manufacturing productivity.

Along with the globalization of the American economy, this drop in productivity did much to undermine the social arrangement by which the postwar era had defined its well-being. No longer was the growth coalition, consisting of big government, labor, and corporate management, able to provide both high corporate profits and a decent level of mass consumption without some kind of industrial policy, which most corporate managers vehemently opposed. What soon followed was a significant loss of manufacturing jobs in the country's industrial heartland, at a time when the real wages and purchasing power of blue-collar workers had already started to decline. Such was the harsh new reality facing organized labor as it prepared its political agenda in early 1977, while expecting that Jimmy Carter and his fellow Democrats would keep their campaign promises made during the 1976 campaign.

Although Carter was disposed to follow a fairly conservative fiscal policy, he, like most other Democrats, seemed willing to go along with George Meany by supporting common situs legislation. A key item on labor's legislative agenda, it was designed to legalize the right of unions, in the words of business historian David Vogel, "to picket an entire construction site in a dispute with any individual contractor working at the site—a practice outlawed by the Supreme Court in 1951." Although the House had passed common situs legislation by a wide margin during the Ford years, it voted on March 23, 1977, by a margin of 217 to 205, to shelve that same bill. Thus, labor suffered its worst defeat on Capitol Hill since its failure to push through a repeal of the Taft-Hartley Act in 1949. Outflanked and outmaneuvered by business, it now faced a serious challenge to its entire agenda from a source that had been passive in recent years.

Business had gone to work once it realized that Gerald Ford's veto was no longer there to deflect a series of congressional challenges to its power coming from regulatory-minded liberals. Hence, corporate-sponsored lobbyists, fearing a further erosion of business's political base on Capitol Hill, organized grass-roots pressure back home to oppose that legislation; they also lobbied hard in Washington. Their effort produced good results, for a number of recently elected Democratic representatives, who had received labor's endorsement in 1976, voted against common situs legislation. Clearly, then, the fight over this bill marked the beginning of a successful business mobilization against a liberal agenda that in time would change the political balance of power and ideological orientation of the 95th Congress.

Business met this challenge to its political influence in ways that revealed a growing tactical sophistication about how to go about winning friends and influencing people. Because unity was the key to success, representatives of large and small firms, including the Business Roundtable and the National Federation of Independent Business, often formed coalitions that allowed them to approach Congress in a more systematic and disciplined manner. Given that changed political approach, labor lost the majorities it once took for granted when the Democrats were in control of Congress.

Ironically, the House of Representatives itself made it easier for business to triumph. After 1974, it responded to calls for reform issued by the liberal interest group Common Cause by altering its rules of procedure governing committee assignments, thereby allowed incoming freshmen to accumulate power and prestige generally at the expense of current committee chairmen. This development weakened labor's standing because it came at a time when a majority of those chairmen in the House still favored a labor-liberal agenda.

As the door now opened for the creation of more power bases in the House, no one was more appreciative of that opportunity than newly elected congressman Richard Gephardt of St. Louis, who represented a largely white middle-class district far removed from the problems and concerns of the inner city and the labor movement. As Gephardt put it, "You know, there is nothing the leadership can offer me, really nothing." That remark captured well the problem faced by House Speaker Thomas "Tip" O'Neill, a New Deal Democrat, who no longer had the political muscle of his predecessors, such as Sam Rayburn, to extract a high degree of loyalty and cooperation from members of his caucus. The decline in the importance of seniority now meant that representatives like Gephardt were in a position to move independently of the House leadership, making them more receptive to political pressures (and more responsive to campaign contributions) coming from both the middle class and business sectors of their local communities.

The fact that some Democrats elected in 1976 were amenable to such local pressure was an important development, which shrewd business lobbyists quickly recognized and then exploited to weaken even further labor's bargaining position in the House. By the late seventies, business organizations, recognizing the importance of grassroots lobbying, were pumping almost a billion dollars a year into an effort to mobilize support for their programs and issues. With that kind of financing, they were able to generate thousands of phone calls and to produce tons of mail so that the voice of the people, or some people, could be properly heard on Capitol Hill. By 1978, the AFL-CIO no longer had the means to counteract such well-organized power flowing from the boardrooms of corporate America.

Jimmy Carter's voice was clearly heard in Washington, but as a result of Watergate and the decline of the Imperial presidency, it did not command the kind of automatic respect that had been accorded to several of his recent predecessors in their relations with Congress. An outsider who had won the office by running against the Washington establishment, he had not endeared himself to important people in Congress. Yet he had a program and a desire to see it enacted into law by Congress. During his first two years in office, he generally supported labor's agenda and the objectives of the public interest lobby, including the creation of the Consumer Protection Agency and the strengthening of the regulatory powers of the Federal Trade Commission. But a massive business mobilization made it difficult for him to get his legislative package through Congress, and he himself would eventually bend to that same pressure.

Carter's problems with Congress went deeper than the lack of an insider's knowledge about how Washington really worked. He had taken office at a time when the decomposition of the national Democratic party was already well advanced, and when liberal economic policies were no longer able to generate noninflationary growth, jobs, and profits. In short, a convergence of factors having to do with the particular character of the Democratic party, as well as the larger structural dynamics of the American political economy, produced a crisis of the welfare state that was impossible for Jimmy Carter to resolve or transcend.

"The original strength of Democratic liberalism was its capacity to build majorities out of minorities," Thomas and Mary Edsall have written. But by the mid-seventies, that liberal coalition had fragmented into several overlapping and often competing interest groups, with each one proposing a separate agenda inside the larger body of liberalism. Blacks, Jews, women, organized labor, and environmentalists now spoke for their own special concerns. Thus, in many cases, a left-liberal social agenda, which included a commitment to affirmative action programs for blacks and women and support for such feminist causes as the Equal Rights Amendment and abortion on de mand, was pushed by people who were, at the same time, committed to the principle that "the personal is political." But because they lacked a larger purpose and one voice, these elements of a fraying Democratic coalition did not offer a program with which a majority of voters could identify; nor did they propose a cogent defense of a general interest that would address the larger concerns of society, especially at a time of widespread social malaise and growing group conflict. In time, conservatives would make political capital by attacking such groups, which had flowered inside the McGovern movement, as "special interest" Democrats.

That ideological and political fragmentation notwithstanding, those associated with a left-liberal social agenda managed to win battles through either the court system or various governmental bureaucracies. Feminists, for example, had scored a major victory in *Roe v. Wade;* blacks had been helped by government-sponsored affirmative action programs, and environmentalists had achieved some success via the regulatory process. But conservatives, who excelled at playing the new politics of old values, questioned and challenged their gains. Thus, when a backlash against an intrusive and allegedly insensitive government gathered growing national support in the late seventies, it was also directed against a legal and administrative liberalism that was not always sanctioned by the court of public opinion or a political majority working through the legislative process.

Yet no matter how discordant or divisive was the debate over social issues, it was overshadowed by the state of the economy. Poll data indicated that in 1979 nearly 70 percent now identified the economic issue as the most important one facing the country, while less than 10 percent focused on social issues. Back in 1970, according to sociologist Jerome Himmelstein, a majority of Americans identified one social issue or another as the country's most salient problem, with only 10 percent pointing to the economy.

Thus Jimmy Carter, apart from having to confront a decaying party system and a shifting political tide, also had to face the reality that the American economy was simply not as productive as it had been in the recent past. Growth rates were down and profit margins had shrunk dramatically; inflation had not appreciably declined; and unemployment was still much higher than any administration could have politically tolerated for long in the sixties or even the early seventies. In short, the politics of stable growth, which had allowed the Democratic party to serve as the champion of both corporate America and social decency, no longer seemed to work in the new age of limits. Consequently, Carter, like any other politician caught in a particularly difficult position, zigged and zagged, hoping to maintain the tenuous coalition that had elected him president in 1976.

Trying to balance those disparate interests, Carter attempted to make trade-offs. He went along with a liberal policy agenda while publicly asserting that governmental spending was contributing to inflation and that the government could not solve all problems. Upon hearing that last remark, Republican senator Howard Baker, the Senate's minority leader, commented that "he is singing our song . . . a Republican song." While Carter tried to sing a Republican song with a Democratic voice and vice versa, he worried most of all about inflation. Nevertheless, he still managed to produce sufficient growth to reduce unemployment by 2 percent between the end of 1976 and the beginning of 1979. Although that success obviously strengthened his hand with a core working-class constituency inside the Democratic party, only one in four voters was more concerned about unemployment than about inflation, while two-thirds saw inflation as the more serious problem. Their respective concerns reflected a distinct class bias: the higher one's income level, the greater one's fear of inflation. In occupational terms, a white collar-managerial stratum wanted to do battle against inflation; blue-collar workers feared unemployment more. As journalist E. J. Dionne, Jr., suggested, "The politics of jobs and the politics of inflation translate[d] into the same thing: the politics of class."

Carter's struggle to cope with inflation was deeply rooted in the realities of presidential politics. As he surely knew, inflation had a depressing impact on the psychological outlook and future expectations of middle-class voters, who certainly would hold a sitting president accountable if their economic prospects were in any way diminished. Coupled with the likelihood of that reaction is the fact that inflation itself was not exactly a polarizing issue. Although Democrats, more than Republicans, generally wanted to lower unemployment, even they, like Republicans and independents, were disposed to deal more decisively with inflation than unemployment. And since a Democratic president had to manage the economy better than a Republican in order to achieve a comparable standing in the polls, there was an added burden on him to produce positive results when confronting inflation. Otherwise, he would alienate not only many partisan Democrats but also a very important and substantial bloc of independent voters whose choice for president could very well decide the outcome of a close election.

Fortunately for Carter, the business cycle seemed to be working to his advantage after 1976: the economy grew at a 4 percent annual rate; inflation ran at just over 6 percent in 1977–78; and unemployment dropped from 7.7 percent in 1976 to 6.1 percent in 1978. But Carter's dealings with Congress were less satisfactory. As a result of a massive business mobilization that was gaining momentum in 1978, he was beginning to face stiff opposition to his domestic program. In Congress, administration supporters faced well-organized opponents who used their skills to block legislation wanted by organized labor and the public interest movement. The struggle to enact these proposals, along with their resultant defeat, constituted a pivotal moment in the political history of the late seventies, indicating that a high tide of conservatism was beginning to roll in toward shore.

The demise of the liberal agenda was a devastating blow to those Democrats who thought they had the votes and the clout to overcome any conservative challenge to their hegemony in Congress. Yet, by 1978, they no longer had the political resources or the will to translate their numerical advantages into solid legislative victories for causes to which they had been traditionally committed. In short, as a result of a conservative mobilization undertaken by business, their opponents had become strong enough to move the legislative agenda to the right, which, in turn, was also a response to, and a reflection of, the changing political attitudes in the country.

Although the public thought that the welfare state was necessary and desirable, there had been a major change in the general outlook of many middle-class voters as to how far the government should intervene in the actual day-to-day affairs of the economy. They now felt that the economy was suffering from excessive governmental regulation during a period of chronic stagflation. Fearing that further governmental intervention might jeopardize their jobs and careers, they rejected what had been acceptable public policy in the early seventies. Before long, their concerns would be felt in Washington.

Many voters also felt that taxes were too high and, worse, that they were being used to support an inefficient, heavily bureaucratized government, which was wasting gobs of money on ill-conceived and ill-managed social programs for the black poor. That perception, coupled with the mounting resistance to more regulation from Washington and a continuing fear of inflation, fueled a backlash against liberalism that by 1978 was hard to resist either in the White House or on Capitol Hill.

A clear indication of that change in the political climate of the day was revealed in the struggle to pass labor reform legislation. A modest bill designed to bring about corporate compliance with existing rules and regulations administered by the National Labor Relations Board, it had easily passed the House and awaited action in the Senate. But in the spring of 1978, Republican senator Orrin Hatch led a well-organized filibuster to defeat all efforts to bring the measure to a successful floor vote. He was ably assisted in this effort by a coalition of business groups, representing both the Business Council and the National Federation of Independent Business, which provided ample resources for this struggle.

That outcome was more than just another triumph for business per se; it also marked a turning point in corporate America's relations with organized labor. No longer would cooperation and the search for consensus characterize labor-management relations; and no longer would wage hikes in a period of declining corporate profits be taken for granted. Thus, those relatively solid working arrangements, which labor and blue-ribbon corporations had fashioned in an earlier period of sustained growth and high productivity, now gave way to a far more conflict-ridden relationship, spelling an end to the period of cooperation that George Meany had found so beneficial for his organization. Outraged by what had happened in the Senate, he later blasted Jimmy Carter for not providing the leadership required to overcome that filibuster.

Labor's defeat in this instance was also matched by the gutting of the Humphrey-Hawkins Bill, which was passed in a form that was very different from what its sponsors had anticipated at the start of the 95th Congress. The key spoke in the liberal wheel, it was substantially modified both as a result of hard pressure applied by Senator Hatch and his supporters and by the willingness of the White House to accept a proposal emphasizing the point that the quest for a full employment economy could not be undertaken unless or until inflation itself was defeated.

Carter's retreat on the Humphrey-Hawkins Bill went along with his stand on fiscal and tax policies. His growing fear of inflation, coupled with the increasing political pressures that he faced from business as well as from many voters, pushed him and other Democrats well to the right of traditional mainstream Democratic positions. And those pressures were intense. By the summer of 1978, the country was so seized by a balanced budget mania that a Democratic Senate endorsed a resolution calling for a balanced budget by 1981. A Gallup Poll of that same year showed that 81 percent of the country favored the adding of a balanced budget amendment to the Constitution. A year later, twenty-nine states out of a necessary thirty-four had endorsed the convening of a constitutional convention to consider such a move.

The argument often advanced by advocates of such strong measures to contain spending was that the federal deficit was responsible for producing inflation, an argument that Carter himself seemed to believe. Although there was very little empirical evidence to support such a claim, the widespread belief that it was so gave politicians, led by California governor Jerry Brown and Ronald Reagan, a chance to score points at the expense of those liberal economists such as Walter Heller or Kenneth Arrow who argued otherwise.

If the Democrats accommodated those demands for a balanced budget, they would be giving away what had been in their long-term interests to defend: the right to use federal funds in such a way as to promote efforts to create a full employment economy as well as to protect the special needs of the poor and the unemployed. A basic tool in the party's kit, intelligently managed deficits had at one time helped to strengthen its ties with such core constituencies as large numbers of skilled and semiskilled blue-collar workers. On the other hand, the combination of inflation and the constant reality of higher taxes had eroded that relationship with many of those same workers, who fiercely resented having to pay for poverty programs, which, they believed, were wasted on a growing underclass of black Americans.

As a result of the prosperity of the sixties and early seventies, a considerable number of workers, now better off than ever before, had altered their social outlook. Douglas Fraser, one-time president of the United Auto Workers, caught that shift even among members of his own progressive union. As he remarked, "The most disturbing thing about it, and I wish it weren't true, is that when people become affluent, their values change. They don't think they should be paying taxes to support people who are less well off."

Meanwhile, the threat of rising inflation and budget deficits forced Carter to backtrack from previously held positions. Consequently, he announced in October 1978 that he was cutting back on spending commitments and would rely on a system of voluntary labor-management agreements to hold down price and wage hikes that went beyond governmentally designated guidelines. While productivity dropped and inflation climbed to an annual average rate of 9 percent in 1978, his efforts to cure the disease of stagflation seemed mired in futility.

While Carter seemed at a loss to find a solution to the country's economic ills, the movement to cut taxes swelled. Although Americans paid a smaller proportion of their earned income on taxes than citizens of virtually all other industrial nations, the combination of stagnating incomes, resentment directed against the inefficiencies of government, and "bracket creep" hit home. Thus, the tax revolt of 1978 became a dominant issue of the day, bringing together diverse groups and interests that otherwise had little in common. And Republicans such as Congressman Jack Kemp and Senator William Roth understood better than Jimmy Carter that this was an issue whose time had come. Their call for lower taxes had provided them with an opportunity to launch a major ideological and political attack on the "tax and spend" policies of the Democrats. As unleashed by the GOP, the politics of taxation fused a number of different concerns of the polity, including antiwelfarism and hostility to government, and it was destined to have a major impact on governmental policy and presidential politics in the years ahead.

Ironically, Carter himself had denounced the existing tax system during the 1976 campaign, charging that it was a "disgrace to the human race." Hence, he asked Congress in early 1978 to consider a tax package that retained many progressive features so characteristic of earlier Democratic legislation. Seeking an increase in a capital gains tax and a reduction in the amount business could claim for certain expenses, Carter stirred up a hornet's nest at a time when there was no significant constituency for tax reform in Washington. While Carter's proposals went nowhere, Congress, operating under intense pressure from business, moved to lower the tax on capital gains, which was something that not even Richard Nixon had been willing to support. In addition, corporate rates were reduced and a 10 percent tax credit for investment was made permanent. All in all, the 1978 Revenue Act was a disaster for liberals; their policy agenda had been turned upside down, and their once-secure control of the legislative agenda had been successfully challenged by a coalition of Republicans and many recently elected Democrats.

That coalition's triumph was made easier as a result of an important vote in California, on June 6, 1978, which happened to coincide with the current tax debate in Washington. On that day, voters approved Proposition 13, which had as its major objective the reduction of property taxes for a populace in search of tax relief. Proposition 13 was on the ballot because a big jump in state and local taxes had placed a heavy burden on the backs of many working people, helping to fuel a statewide tax revolt that resulted from an 84.6 percent increase in the assessed value of single-family homes between 1975 and 1978. But after Governor Jerry Brown refused to spend any of the $5 billion surplus in the state treasury for tax relief, California voters soon sent a message loud and clear across the country, which went far to accelerate and to justify the push in Washington and elsewhere for changes in the current tax structure.

Among the chief beneficiaries of the 1978 Revenue Act were investors and property-owning Americans, who by 1980 received an extra $5.5 billion dollars of tax relief from Washington. But many middle-class and working-class Americans, who favored the continuation of governmental services, while condemning governmental mismanagement and bloat, were caught in the coils of an ever more regressive taxation system. Higher Social Security taxes, combined with bracket creep, had placed a heavy tax load on their backs, making them in time far more sympathetic to demands from conservative ideologues for "tax reform." (Ironically, when tax legislation was passed during the Reagan years, it benefited precisely those people who already possessed the most wealth and power in America.)

That 1978 was a difficult year for regulatory-minded liberals was further confirmed by congressional rejection of a Carter-endorsed proposal for a consumer protection agency. Since 1972, the House had supported the creation of such an agency on three separate occasions. Now, a well-organized effort by business to derail this proposal, combined with a growing hostility on the grass-roots level to more governmental bureaucracy, turned that vote around. A substantial number of freshman Democrats deserted the White House, thereby spelling defeat for Carter and the House Democratic leadership as well.

An even worse setback for supporters of the regulatory state occurred when the House refused to endorse a conference committee report that would have authorized the Federal Trade Commission to extend its jurisdictional reach over business. Once again, the House responded to grass-roots pressure. According to David Vogel, complaints about this legislation poured into Washington from "funeral directors, from used car dealers, and their optometrists and their doctors and dentists and everybody else." Efforts by the House leadership to overcome that political mobilization were soundly rebuffed, given such a strong protest from people with standing back home.

Middle-class voters no longer favored greater governmental regulation of the economy at a time of perceived economic crisis and uncertainty. Hence, they turned their back on a public interest agenda that had received their support before the stagflation of the late seventies had become such a depressing reality. And they now agreed with the arguments advanced by business spokesmen that the costs of regulation were not only excessive but harmful to growth itself.

The results of the 1978 midterm election confirmed that voters had turned to the right, away from even the cautious centrism of Jimmy Carter. That trend to the right was already clearly established during the primaries, as a number of liberal Democrats and moderate to liberal Republicans succumbed to a conservative avalanche inside their respective parties. In Massachusetts, for example, Governor Michael Dukakis lost a primary race to conservative Edward King, which foreshadowed the politics of the eighties. King's campaign staff picked up ground by focusing voters' attention on Dukakis's opposition to a tax cut and his liberal views on abortion and capital punishment, which threatened the social values and beliefs of lower-middle-class or working-class white voters inside his own party. A devastating defeat for Dukakis, it indicated that the politics of cultural resentment had become a lethal weapon, even in the one state that George McGovern had won in 1972.

Liberal Republican senator Clifford Case of New Jersey also lost his primary battle to Jeffrey Bell, a leading spokesman for New Right causes. At a time when the regular Republican party organization was inert, Bell was helped by the activism and commitment of conservative supporters, who provided him a narrow primary victory over the longtime Republican incumbent. Although Bell lost in November to Democrat Bill Bradley, he had served the cause of the right by unseating an establishment liberal whose views were anathema to Bell's supporters inside the Republican party.

In November, Case was joined in retirement by a number of Democratic Senate liberals, who were also defeated by Republican conservatives blessed with ample money, organizational skills, and an ideological zeal very few Democrats could hope to match. Iowa's Dick Clark, New Hampshire's Thomas McIntyre, and Colorado's Floyd Haskell were each retired as a result of a strong conservative mobilization in their respective states. In Iowa, Roger Jepsen benefited enormously from the support he received from a highly energized pro-life bloc, which committed its resources and votes to him. In addition, Jepsen won statewide support by attacking Clark for having voted for the Panama Canal treaties, which many conservatives, including Ronald Reagan, had denounced as a sellout of basic American interests and a betrayal of fundamental American values. Aided by a number of single issue groups, including pro-lifers, Jepsen managed to put together a conservative coalition that defeated Clark by twenty-six thousand votes.

Jepsen's defeat of Clark, reputed to be the most liberal senator in the upper chamber, was no election year anomaly. In Colorado, fellow liberal Floyd Haskell was unseated by conservative William Armstrong, who attacked him as another eastern elitist out of touch with the values of mainstream opinion in that state. In New Hampshire, incumbent Thomas McIntyre lost a close race to Gordon Humphrey, an organizer for the Conservative Caucus. Running what McIntyre later described as a vicious campaign, Humphrey pulled out all the stops to defeat his opponent. He effectively mobilized grassroots groups in a generally conservative state to win another Senate seat for the Republican right by turning McIntyre's votes for the Panama Canal treaties against him.

Voter apathy was rife in 1978, as less than 38 percent of eligible voters managed to go to the polls; but the results in these three states and elsewhere provided striking evidence that the rout of liberals and the repudiation of their causes was now well under way throughout the nation. Not only did longtime liberals lose seats in both the House and the Senate to very conservative Republicans, whose numbers in both chambers were increasing rapidly, but California governor Jerry Brown won a big reelection victory by campaigning for a balanced budget amendment to the Constitution. And Democrat Edward King, with the help of the right, was elected governor of Massachusetts while declaring his opposition to any tax increases for his state.

The results of the 1978 election proved to be significant for three reasons. First, they confirmed that party partisanship was continuing to decline, providing fresh opportunities for campaigners on the political right to make headway for their various causes, including support for prayer in the public schools and opposition to abortion. Second, they strengthened the connection between ideological conservatives, business elites, and the Republican party in ways that proved very advantageous for each group in 1980. And third, they forced Jimmy Carter to move more to the right than was the case during his first two years in the White House.

The administration revealed its hand during a midterm conference of the Democratic party held shortly after the 1978 election. Party liberals, including Senator Edward Kennedy, sought to rally their forces behind a left-liberal-labor program but administration representatives beat back all floor attempts to push the White House in that direction, especially with respect to budget priorities. Their action was a clear indication that Carter was moving with the tide, seeking to protect himself from the charge that he was another irresponsible free-spending liberal. (However pronounced were their differences on many domestic issues, Carter and Kennedy supported moves to deregulate certain sectors of the American economy, including the airline industry.)

Carter's politics of restraint were designed to placate the business community and Wall Street. He and his economic advisers, led by Charles Schultze, now shared the view that an expansive fiscal policy had exacerbated the problem of inflation and weakened the dollar in international money markets. They thought a cutback in federal spending and a reduction in the deficit would lower the inflation rate, create a healthier environment for investment from the private sector at home, and strengthen the dollar abroad. But whether their approach provided the right answers to the problem of stagflation was another matter.

There was little or no evidence that deficits per se actually produced inflation. Furthermore, the money saved from such proposed cutbacks would be at best negligible, and it would come from the welfare sector of the budget, ensuring that the weakest and most needy of Americans would have to pay for a policy designed to placate business. And the generalized fear that excessive governmental spending had crowded out private investors and contributed to a capital shortage was unfounded. *Business Week*, for example, reported in

September 1978 that the 545 largest American corporations had accumulated $80 billion, which they simply refused to spend.

While the debate about the administration's budget priorities heated up inside the Democratic party, the existing budget deficit was coming down, dropping from $66 billion in 1976 to $27.7 billion in 1979. Furthermore, the percentage of the goods and services purchased by the government, in terms of its share of the GNP, also declined, as did the government's share of the growing national debt, which now stood at less than 20 percent of the total figure. These figures showed that in proportional terms the government's overall relationship to the debt structure of the larger economy had improved slightly during the Carter years.

Still, there had been increased funding for governmental transfer payments, now amounting to an estimated 12.5 percent of the GNP for the 1979–81 period. They had provided needed assistance to the elderly and funding for many public infrastructure programs and projects, taking the form of Social Security payouts and grants-in-aid to the states and municipalities. But a big jump in inflation in early 1979 made those programs increasingly vulnerable to budget cuts of some kind. Since he was preparing to raise the level of military spending, Carter asked Congress to consider the elimination of "unnecessary" Social Security benefits. And he would later seek a reduction in funds for grants-in-aid to the states and municipalities.

Carter's emerging attack on the welfare state was supported by key Democrats on Capitol Hill, indicating that the fear of inflation and voter retribution had forced the party to retreat both ideologically and programmatically from that brand of Keynesian liberalism with which it had long been identified. Campaign contributions from business and intense grass-roots pressure from voters had played a major role in promoting such a shift. Fed up with rising taxes and stagnating incomes, those voters opposed any more spending on social programs, which they felt were not needed or wanted. The convergence of those two points of view was sufficient to change the political context in which most Democratic politicians now had to operate.

A similar development had already occurred in Britain. In early 1979, the Tories, led by Margaret Thatcher, replaced a Labour government that could not curb an inflationary spiral undermining the living standards of British workers and the middle class. In his study tracing the rise of Thatcherism, Peter Jenkins captured the dilemma facing not only British Social Democrats but, indirectly, American liberals as well: "What was happening in Britain was part of a world-wide phenomenon: everywhere in the industrialised democratic world the old manual working class was in decline, trade union membership was falling, old class loyalties were crumbling. . . . In part democratic socialism was the victim of its own success. The welfare societies it had helped to build had opened other and less-collectivist avenues of advancement. Affluence had eaten into old class loyalties. Education had provided ladders of escape from the working class. But democratic socialism—or, in the continental usage, social democracy, was inflationary."

In a sense, the American welfare state could be construed as inflationary, insofar as it provided a vast array of financial supports and investment incentives that a corporate capitalist economy needed for survival. But although very few Americans wanted to change that relationship, many were decidedly unhappy with the pricing policy of the oil majors, which, they felt, had taken full advantage of a genuine or contrived gasoline shortage to profit at their expense. Whether or not those firms had so profited, the politics of oil and the concomitant energy crisis brought home, to one and all, the increasing vulnerability of the American system to forces and interests beyond the reach of American power to alter significantly for the better. In short, the 1979 Iranian Revolution, coupled with the most recent OPEC price hike, was stark evidence of that new reality.

Carter tried to cope with the domestic implications of the energy crisis by offering a package that he hoped would placate the many interest groups involved with the production and consumption of those precious resources. Earlier, he had promised the oil industry during the 1976 campaign that if elected he would seek to deregulate natural gas prices. But he was also aware of consumer needs, so he went back on his word, angering many powerful people in the business, who were not pleased, either, with his efforts to push for energy conservation. Later, with his approval, Congress passed legislation that allowed all newly discovered natural gas to be deregulated by 1985.

In April 1979, Carter announced a gradual decontrol of prices on domestic oil in an attempt to stimulate domestic production. At the same time, he sought to impose a windfall profits tax on all domestically produced crude, a move that outraged the many independent oil producers, who already had reason to dislike him. Although Congress passed legislation in 1980 that placed a windfall tax on the majors at a higher rate than the independents, it was now too late for the White House to make amends to the domestic industry. The political damage having been done, the independent oil producers, working with conservative Republicans across the country, prepared to spend millions in the 1980 election to defeat Carter and as many liberals in Congress as their money and connections would permit.

In the meantime, OPEC raised the price on a barrel of imported oil to just over $14, which nearly doubled the previous asking price. Even before that news broke in June 1979, motorists across the United States lined up at the gas pumps, hoping to avoid a shortage that many believed was being arranged by the oil companies to boost their profits. Aware of the growing public outrage, Carter sought to defuse the damage at a time when his standing in the polls indicated that his chances of winning reelection in 1980 were poor indeed. He addressed the country in mid-July 1979, attributing the prevalent sour mood to a "crisis of confidence," which, in his words, was "threatening to destroy the political and social fabric of America." And he advised his fellow citizens not to look to Washington for solutions to their problems; they could only be found by the people themselves. America, he suggested, could overcome that "crisis of confidence" by once more restoring traditional values of hard work, the family, the community, and "faith in God" to their proper place in the country's scheme of things. This was Carter's admonition to the American people as he sought to confront rhetorically a situation that the energy crisis had exacerbated but by itself had not created.

The malaise of the late seventies, which Carter discussed in his speech, had called into question the old political and economic arrangements whereby the Democratic party maintained a sufficient degree of economic growth and prosperity to keep its coalition intact. But the combination of growing unemployment and higher inflation, along with the racial and cultural tensions inside the Democratic party, exacerbated a political situation for which Carter had no immediate solution. Conservatives, on the other hand, moved ahead, growing in confidence, organizational strength, and appeal. They tapped into powerful feelings associated with American nationalism and patriotism by crucifying Carter for allegedly selling out the Panama Canal. In addition, they attacked him as a weak leader in the fight against communism, charging that his commitment to the SALT process demonstrated that he lacked the will and toughness to defend vital American interests in a dangerous world. At home, conservatives capitalized on rampant inflation and the continuing loss of jobs by pointing to high taxes and governmental regulation as the agents most responsible for declining economic growth and productivity. They denounced Great Society programs as a waste of taxpayer dollars. They opposed all forms of preferential hiring, charging that this approach undermined the American tradition of fair play and equal opportunity in the marketplace. And they assailed the liberalism of the Supreme Court, which, in their view, had opened the door to abortion and pornography and closed it to prayer in the public schools. These, then, were the domestic and international issues that conservatives used in an effort to mobilize a mass base for Ronald Reagan's 1980 presidential campaign.

Faced with mounting opposition from all sides, Carter sought to reassure a majority of middle-class voters by opting to fight inflation rather than to support the goals of a full employment economy. But his "strategy of restraint" ran the risk of alienating those black and white voters who had supported him in 1976 in the belief that the Democratic party could still create jobs and a secure future for their families. But if they were to remain loyal to the national Democratic party, Carter would have to deliver something more than the politics of austerity. Otherwise he might suffer the embarrassment of a challenge from Senator Edward Kennedy, who was currently the candidate of choice among Democrats by a margin of better than two to one.

Seeking to confront the crisis that was eroding his presidency, Carter moved in late July 1979 to reassure both Wall Street and the international financial community that he meant business. Hence, he appointed Paul Volcker the new chairman of the Federal Reserve Board. A tough-minded monetarist, whose many years of governmental service went back to the Kennedy administration, Volcker would not hesitate to use all of his awesome powers to regulate the money supply and interest rates in order to defeat inflation. In fact, just before announcing Volcker's appointment, Carter had been warned by his friend Bert Lance that Volcker's policies would lead to higher interest rates and higher unemployment, which then might "mortgage" his reelection chances in 1980 to the Federal Reserve Board.

Carter now awaited results from Volcker at a time when the annual inflation rate had jumped to 14 percent in the late summer of 1979. Ironically, Volcker gave Carter more than he bargained for. By October 1979, it was clear to the White House that Volcker was determined to fight inflation with his own strategy of restraint, which was far more ruthless and politically insensitive than anyone had anticipated. Volcker was going to confront the ogre of inflation directly in order to protect the American dollar abroad and to instill financial discipline at home. Consequently, he raised interest rates and reduced the money supply sufficiently to lay the groundwork for a "Carter" recession, which went far in 1980 to provide the Republican Right with the frosting on the political cake it had been baking since the mid-seventies.

Inflation notwithstanding, Carter had benefited from a period of solid economic growth during his first two years in office. Since a downturn of some kind was inevitable, he had been advised to take it in 1979 in order to avoid the more serious repercussion of a recession in an election year. But Carter dismissed that sound advice, thereby giving a strong-minded Paul Volcker his opportunity to drive the economic agenda on his terms and with his own sense of timing. Carter, wanting it both ways, was now trapped by a situation he and his closest advisers had not foreseen when Volcker was appointed chairman in late July 1979.

The last two months of 1979 brought only more bad news for the president. Senator Edward Kennedy announced that he would seek the Democratic nomination in 1980; the shock troops of the Iranian Revolution seized the American Embassy in Teheran, along with fifty-three hostages, after Carter allowed the deposed Shah of Iran to enter the United States for medical treatment; and the Russians invaded Afghanistan, which effectively destroyed what was left of the detente era of the seventies.

As it turned out, Kennedy did not seriously threaten Carter, although he further weakened him at a time when the Republicans were on the march. The harsh memory of Chappaquiddick, plus Kennedy's reputation as a welfare state liberal, helped Carter win key Democratic primaries. In addition, he benefited enormously from the rally-around-the-president mood, which both the hostage affair and the Soviet invasion of Afghanistan had engendered.

Although Carter successfully undermined Kennedy's candidacy by concentrating on foreign policy issues and avoiding a debate with him, his many problems did not go away. In April 1980, he was hurt by a botched military operation to free the hostages, which led Secretary of State Cyrus Vance to resign as a protest against the president's failure to tell him in advance that the mission had been given his final approval. Long after Vance's departure, the hostages were still being held in Teheran, becoming for many Americans an aggravating symbol of the country's further loss of power and respect in a post-Vietnam world.

In addition, the Russian move into Afghanistan in late 1979 seriously damaged Soviet-American relations. Saying that the Russian invasion was the worst thing to happen since World War II, Carter responded by authorizing a major buildup of American strategic forces and by launching an ideological crusade in the spirit of the cold war. He embargoed the shipment of grain to the Soviet Union and refused to allow the United States to participate in the 1980 Moscow Olympics. Trying in every conceivable way to deflect the charge from conservatives that he was a weak and spineless president, Carter even went so far as to proclaim his own strategic doctrine for the Middle East, and he later issued a presidential directive that authorized the creation of a limited nuclear war capability.

Carter acted out of a sense of desperation as he sought to fashion a credible foreign policy that could be used in the fall campaign against a possible Republican conservative. In the spring of 1980, he also had to deal with inflation. But because he was unable to raise taxes and unwilling to impose price and wage controls, Carter confronted his number one domestic problem by reducing funding for welfare programs. At a time when an actual recession was under way, he deliberately sought to cut the budget deficit for the purpose of freeing funds for capital investment in the private sector. When the Democratic leaders in Congress joined him in pursuit of a balanced budget for fiscal year 1981, it was a pivotal moment in the history of postwar liberalism.

By the summer of 1980, the liberal agenda of the sixties was in a desiccated political and intellectual state, as the Democrats under Carter had moved to the right. Labor's dramatic loss of countervailing political power, coupled with increasingly well-targeted corporate campaign financing, played an important role in promoting that shift. In addition, the tax revolt from the grass roots and a growing hostility to big government also scared many Democrats who otherwise might have continued their support for programs designed to help the poor and needy.

But an even more fundamental process was at work: The American economy was suffering from serious stagflation for which the Democrats had no solution. Hence, they could no longer play their kind of politics, which had been predicated on economic growth and an optimistic belief in a bright future. In short, the new politics of austerity all but precluded legislative deals that included benefits for the rich, the middle class, and the poor alike.

Since the forties, the Democratic party had been the party of good times. Under its aegis, corporate America prospered; organized labor, along with the racial and ethnic minorities, also benefited. Once the cultural and racial strife of the sixties and seventies fed into the economic downturn of the late seventies, however, Jimmy Carter and his fellow Democrats were at a loss to find the means of overcoming that political fragmentation which had virtually destroyed their once-proud coalition of North and South, black and white, haves and have-nots. By 1980 the liberal center, lacking both intellectual coherence and a viable political and economic strategy, confronted a conservative movement ready and eager to challenge it for power.

4

The Triumph of
Conservatism, 1980

—————————

—————————

As Jimmy Carter's standing with the public eroded after 1977, conservative Republicans sensed that a door of political opportunity had opened for people of their persuasion. Encouraged by Ronald Reagan's strong showing in the fight for the 1976 Republican nomination, they looked forward to taking control not only of the party but of the White House as well. So while Reagan, their putative leader, waited in the wings to launch his 1980 campaign for the presidency, they intensified their attack on Carter's foreign and domestic programs, offering policies and programs of their own making in order to restore American economic power at home and political prestige and pride abroad.

Part of that conservative assault on what they saw as Carter's liberal agenda came from the direction of the New Right, which had much in common with a slightly older generation of right-wing activists or critics. Since the fifties and sixties, conservatives had opposed a policy of detente with the Soviet Union, and they consistently denounced the taxing policies of big government and the inefficiencies and waste of the welfare state, not to speak of such liberal causes as forced busing and the Equal Rights Amendment.

Although such views had become the cornerstone of the conservative faith for both the Old and the New Right, the changing political and economic environment of the late seventies provided New Right organizers, led by Richard Viguerie and Paul Weyrich, with an opportunity to mobilize opposition to abortion and to encourage support for prayer in the public schools. Ideological militants with an anti-establishment message, they found receptive audiences everywhere in the country, not just in the Sunbelt.

For those militants, the stakes in this struggle were high. As sociologist James D. Hunter points out, they were engaged in a cultural civil war with their liberal adversaries over such matters as the definition of the family, the content of public education, the role of the media in shaping or altering popular culture, and the various court decisions affecting personal values. Battling, then, to define "the meaning of America" on their terms, they sought to roll back the "rights revolution" and to undermine the moral legitimacy of their opponents as well. Thus, their efforts transcended localized or regionalized interests and touched on longstanding national conflicts, which were rooted in the profoundly different belief systems and operating codes separating moral traditionalists from social liberals of a secular persuasion.

As this cultural war heated up in the late seventies, men and women on the right began to achieve success in the political arena. For example, a combination of hard work, ample money, and mastery of the new communications technology helped people like Viguerie and Weyrich to score victories in 1978 in such states as New Hampshire, Colorado, and Iowa. And it now seemed that these New Right activists had suddenly found a home inside the Republican party, contrary to what William Rusher, publisher of the National Review, had thought either possible or desirable in 1976. Rusher, along with Viguerie and Weyrich, had given up on the national Republican party after Richard Nixon and Gerald Ford failed to advance a domestic and foreign policy agenda in keeping with his own views. Viguerie himself had even declared, "I don't believe that in my lifetime you will ever again be able to market the word 'Republican.' You could as easily sell the Edsel or Typhoid Mary." Weyrich, too, had also expressed a similar contempt for the Republican party. But now that the New Right was gaining in strength and confidence, the main beneficiary of that development turned out to be the conservative wing of the Republican party, especially in the Sunbelt.

Southern conservatives had already benefited from the racial fallout resulting from Lyndon Johnson's sponsorship of the civil rights legislation of the sixties; in fact, so many white voters had moved out of the Democratic party that not even Jimmy Carter, a native of Georgia, could win back a white majority in 1976. Also, the suburbanization of Dixie contributed significantly to the realigning process now under way, nurturing not only an antistatist ideology but a fresh leadership cadre for a growing party whose roots had already spread deep into the rich soil of the new business-minded South. Thus, from Richmond to Houston, and from southern Florida to western Tennessee, conservative Republicans from middle-class suburbs had now become a powerful force in the presidential politics of the region.

The politicization of evangelical Protestants by the New Religious Right was another key factor in helping to promote a shift to presidential Republicanism in the South and Southwest. Although the New Religious Right was organizationally and ideologically connected to the secular New Right, it had its own distinctive character, emerging in the late seventies as a result of a number of converging factors. The rapid racial, social, and cultural changes of the sixties and early seventies, including the legalization of abortion and the interdiction of prayer in the public schools, along with the proliferation of pornography and the emergence of the gay and feminist movements, went far to unsettle and disturb millions of citizens.

In addition, the federal government itself played a role in triggering a grass-roots mobilization by the religious right. For instance, both the Federal Communications Commission and the Internal Revenue Service were involved in actions that preachers and their parishioners found threatening. The FCC had put a freeze on granting licenses for religious programming; and in the first year of the Carter administration, the IRS began the process of revoking the tax-exempt status of racially discriminatory private schools.

Although Jimmy Carter had won the votes of some Southern Baptists in 1976, their later disillusionment with him led to a further politicization of the religious right, which drove a permanent wedge between the Carter White House and most evangelicals. They realized that Carter, though a born-again Christian, was unwilling to support or work for their agenda. Carter himself personally opposed abortion, but his administration refused to back a constitutional amendment outlawing it; furthermore, it opposed prayer in the public schools and took the view that to give tax credits to parents whose children went to religious schools was unconstitutional.

Clearly, the tax stance of the IRS had made people like the Reverend Jerry Falwell feel he was in a "fight for our lives." But much more was involved than simply opposing the IRS. At a time when mainstream Protestant denominations were in decline, Southern

Baptist churches were increasing in enrollment, providing the religious right with a growing constituency for the message that the country was suffering from the scourge of "secular humanism." In their view, liberal political and cultural elites had fostered an environment that had allowed crime to flourish, traditional family values to erode, and Soviet power to spread. In short, these same elites, so the charge went, were guilty of undermining the moral fiber of the Republic by secularizing its civil and social institutions and by relativizing standards of ethical judgment.

Among those who sought "to put God back in government" was the Reverend Marion "Pat" Robertson, a leading televangelist who had supported Carter in 1976. After Robertson had broken with Carter, he had become an important figure in the newly created Christian Voice, which sought to grade members of the House and Senate on a variety of social issues of interest to the religious right. Thanks to Robertson's excellent media connections, Christian Voice now had an outlet that gave the adepts of the religious right greater exposure and opportunities for fundraising and social mobilization. But the Moral Majority, founded by the Reverend Falwell in 1979, played a far more important role in forwarding the goals of the religious right. It sought through television appeals and direct mail campaigns to build a national grass-roots network that relied heavily on local Baptist ministers, especially in the South, to advance its program of registering new voters and educating them about the dangers of secular humanism. Falwell later claimed that his organization was responsible for adding over two million new voters to the rolls in 1980.

That attack, which was directed against big government and the Supreme Court, was also supported by such shrewd right-wing political organizers as Howard Phillips and Ed McAteer, who joined forces with Falwell and other preachers of the New Religious Right. In their common effort to politicize evangelicals and fundamentalists, they went far to increase the number of right-wing activists willing to work inside the Republican party. But whether they worked inside or outside the Republican party, their message was the same. As Viguerie himself said, what was new was not what they said but the fact that "conservatives have learned how to recruit, how to organize, and how to successfully market ideas." Given such entrepreneurial skills, sophisticated televangelists like Falwell and Robertson were able to enlist growing grass-roots support and to produce a steady cash flow to help disseminate their views on such matters as abortion and prayer in the public schools. While working with others of similar persuasion, they succeeded in pushing their candidates and agendas inside a party whose political center of gravity was now shifting well to the right of Richard Nixon or even Gerald Ford.

Clearly, the successful marketing of the social issue, which helped to promote that shift, was in line with the geopolitical strategy of Kevin Phillips, who had argued in 1969 that a new national Republican majority could be created by politicizing a conservative populist agenda both in the North and in the South. Although Watergate had temporarily frustrated that opportunity, the pervasive disenchantment with public institutions and opposition to welfare state spending encouraged activists of the New Right to think that something approaching a conservative breakthrough might be under way.

The election results of 1978 went far to raise such expectations: Three new conservatives won Senate seats, and several more were sent to the House. Significantly, many of these victories came about as a result of the coalescing of forces on the right, which brought together various groups that opposed abortion and the Panama Canal treaties, as well as the Equal Rights Amendment and gun control legislation. On the other hand, the political mobilization that took place did not necessarily represent a broad upheaval from below. Rather, it took the more narrow form of creating conservative cadres and cohorts who were willing to promote certain social issues and to find supporters for their respective causes inside a Republican party that was beginning to recover from the debacle of Watergate.

There were also other developments that helped to establish the context for the conservative surge that carried Ronald Reagan to victory in 1980. Among them was a growing intellectual attack on Great Society liberalism that originated with academic journalists who wrote for such publications as *The Public Interest* and *Commentary*. Led by Irving Kristol, Nathan Glazer, and Norman Podhoretz, these neoconservatives—as they were called—did not repudiate the welfare state of New Deal vintage; instead, they opposed, above all, those affirmative action programs that had evolved out of the Great Society, believing that these programs would undermine a basic American principle, equality of opportunity in the marketplace.

At the same time, neoconservatives charged that many governmental programs of the sixties, designed to alleviate poverty and assist the working poor, had failed. Like Richard Nixon, they agreed that throwing more money at programs was not the answer. Hence, they opposed the creation of major new programs to cope with the plight of the American underclass, claiming that adequate governmental solutions and resources were not readily available to deal with a crisis of such magnitude. In addition, they feared that the real object of such programs was to create the basis for an equality of condition, not opportunity, which intellectuals of their bent strongly rejected on both philosophical and political grounds. Although Glazer and Kristol greatly exaggerated the dangers of a radical egalitarianism, they had provided a certain intellectual respectability for the argument that it was more important to accept the limits of current social policy than to expand current governmental welfare policies.

The neoconservative critique of Great Society programs also had political significance, since it reinforced the common belief that inflation was the product of excessive governmental spending, and that one good way to end the government's waste and profligacy (and thereby reduce inflation) was to cut back on spending on unworkable, useless welfare programs. As the calls for fiscal retrenchment filled the air in the mid- and late seventies, it was becoming more and more clear that the drift to conservatism was rooted, in part, in a growing disillusionment with governmental poverty programs, ever-increasing taxes, and the simmering and ill-disguised resentment directed at the black poor by lower-middle-class and working-class whites. This, then, was the context for a 1978 Gallup Poll that reported that 47 percent of the people interviewed now identified themselves as conservatives; 32 percent, liberals; and 10 percent, middle of the roaders. Such data revealed how far the American people had moved from views they had held in the early and mid-sixties, when a majority saw themselves as either liberal or moderate, not conservative, in their political outlook and beliefs.

Working to promote such a shift in views was Irving Kristol, who offered a staunch intellectual defense of the free market. Aware of the subtle role that ideology plays in legitimating elite behavior of various kinds, Kristol sought to secure the high moral ground for corporate America by helping to burnish its image in the political and intellectual marketplace of the country. He repeatedly wrote in the *Wall Street Journal* that huge Keynesian deficits, created by a costly and mismanaged welfare state, along with a tax-gouging, fiscally irresponsible federal government, had made it more difficult for the American economy to remain competitive both at home and in world markets. And he argued that deregulation and, above all, tax cuts were absolutely necessary in order to revive economic growth at home and to restore American primacy in world markets.

Kristol also helped Jude Wanniski, a former *Wall Street Journal* editorial writer, obtain foundation support for the purpose of getting his tax-cutting views published in book form. In 1978, Wanniski's influential tract *The Way the World Works* spelled out what was fast becoming the intellectual rage in conservative circles: the case for supply-side economic theory and practice. The crux of Wanniski's argument was that major cuts in corporate and personal tax rates would go far to stimulate fresh investment and to encourage production and consumption. Such heightened economic activity, he believed, would also restore lost revenue to the government, thereby compensating it for what had been given away through those initial tax cuts.

A clear, uncomplicated economic prescription for overcoming stagflation, Wanniski's approach to policymaking was predicated on Arthur Laffer's famous curve. Laffer, a professor of economics at the University of Southern California, argued that if tax rates were set too high or too low, they would not produce those sought-after objectives of growth and the restoration of lost revenues. But his curve (or graph), which sought to strike the right balance in the tax rate, "neglected to include any numbers." As one historian noted, "It remained anybody's guess what ideal tax rate would both stimulate economic growth and yield sufficient revenues to reduce the deficit." Whether Laffer's curve had any empirical validity was beside the point: with the passage of California's Proposition 13 in June 1978, the tax issue had suddenly caught political fire in Congress and the country; it now seemed that his curve was fast becoming a straight line for politicians to follow.

Consequently, Republican congressman Jack Kemp, converted to the supply-side cause by Wanniski, began to attract attention from many conservative Republicans, who liked his stance on tax cuts (as reflected in the current Kemp-Roth tax bill) as well as the sharp remarks he directed at the Democrats. According to Kemp, the Democrats not only lacked a proper economic understanding of the issues and a suitable program to cope with stagflation, they also were the practitioners of a zero-sum game at home, not the harbingers of growth and prosperity for all. As it turned out, his was the message that the GOP would deliver as a party in 1980, in an attempt to discredit the politics and practice of Keynesian liberalism during a period of major economic turmoil and distress.

While Kemp fought the ideological and legislative battle on behalf of supply-side economics, others were also involved in a related struggle to restore the market to its hallowed and privileged place in American life. Wealthy sponsors such as Joseph Coors and Richard Scaife, along with able administrators like William Baroody, created or operated a dense network of conservative think tanks in Washington and elsewhere. They included the American Enterprise Institute, the Heritage Foundation, and the Hoover Institution, which served as the most important research centers for conservative intellectuals, providing politicians and the media alike with position papers and monographs on a variety of subjects from foreign policy to welfare reform.

The American Enterprise Institute, founded in the 1940s, grew in time into a significant institutional rival to the liberal establishment's Brookings Institution. By the mid-1970s, with financial support provided by leading corporations, it managed to embark on a major campaign to mobilize public opinion on their behalf. In that vein, the AEI published journals such as *Regulation* and *Public Opinion*, sponsored seminars and conferences, and produced reams of material that aired on radio and television. As Baroody put it, "We pay as much attention to dissemination of product as content." And that product was designed to roll back the reach of the regulatory state and to promote the cause of supply-side economics.

The work of the AEI had provided business with useful material in an effort to undermine the consensus that had made possible the regulatory initiatives of the early seventies. For example, Murray Weidenbaum, editor of *Regulation*, argued that an overzealous federal government, ostensibly bent on safeguarding the public's interest, had made it far more costly for business to compete in a global environment. Although his estimates were challenged on grounds that they lacked empirical validityand credibility, corporate America now had data from a respectable source to argue its case that governmental bureaucrats were impeding progress and undermining growth.

The Heritage Foundation was far more explicitly ideological in its approach to policy matters. Created by Edward Feulner and Paul Weyrich in 1973 and funded by Joseph Coors, the beer baron, it spoke not for the Fortune 500 firms but the entrepreneurs of the Sunbelt, that is, the self-made men who eagerly promoted Ronald Reagan's drive for the presidency. In addition to publishing various materials and sponsoring conferences to advance its point of view, the Heritage Foundation was actively involved in the legislative battles on Capitol Hill, where it provided advice and assistance to conservative legislators on a variety of different issues of concern. Heritage's goal was to move people in its direction, because, in the words of its director, "people are policy." Such was the approach of this activist-minded organization as it sought to connect with key people on Capitol Hill and elsewhere who supported its objectives.

The Hoover Institution in Stanford, California, matched in importance those other think tanks in Washington. At Hoover could be found many of the intellectual and academic luminaries of American conservatism, including economist Milton Friedman, who had received the Nobel Prize in Economics in 1976. A staunch advocate of free markets and an opponent of the welfare state, Friedman was a leading conservative economist of his time; his views defending the primacy of the market were presented with a certain verve on television and in print. An equally committed monetarist, he also argued that inflation could be defeated as long as the Federal Reserve Board was willing to pursue a tight money policy no matter how long it took to do the job. In another capacity, Friedman served as a mentor of sorts for Ronald Reagan, who shared his belief that big government had compounded the woes of the American economy, making it more difficult to restore stable growth and to project an optimistic future for Americans.

As Reagan shifted gears to prepare for another run at the White House, it was becoming evident that many more people in the country now shared his opinion that government was the problem, not the solution. Certainly such a point of view was strongly held inside the American business community. Worried about escalating costs, falling productivity, global competition, and excessive governmental intervention, large and small businesses alike sought to change matters by undertaking a well-funded drive to discredit the federal regulatory state; by the late seventies, they had made sufficient headway that liberals inside the Carter administration and Congress lost the power to set the national policy agenda. As a result of a massive business mobilization that coincided with changing national perceptions about the state of the economy and the role of the state, the political context for making policy had changed dramatically since Jimmy Carter had taken office in 1977.

The Business Roundtable, which spoke for elite corporate managers of the United States, was a critical force behind that mobilization. The organizations it now represented had, at one time, accepted
the fact that high wages for American workers and the preservation
of the welfare state served their purposes as well. In short, corporate
America's informal social compact with organized labor, along with
its willingness to tolerate increased governmental funding of the welfare state, helped to swell its profit margins in a period marked by
high domestic consumption, which characterized the sixties and early seventies. Yet those earlier arrangements, which had made possible that remarkable period of prosperity and growth, fell apart by the
late seventies due to the persistence of stagflation and, above all, the
emergence of a globalized economy.

As those corporate managers understood, American business was
now facing serious competition at home and abroad. By 1980, foreign
auto companies had captured 22 percent of the domestic market, representing a 14 percent jump over the figures for 1970 — and steel imports, along with many other items, continued to rise as well. Meanwhile, the American share of world markets for manufacturing goods
had declined by 23 percent in that same decade. Given these current
trends, an overall trade deficit was developing, which would become
a very serious problem for the American economy in the years ahead.
Moreover, by 1980 the United States already had the most obsolete
plants, the lowest percentage of capital investments, and the poorest
rate of economic growth of any important industrial power other
than the United Kingdom. Here, then, was the macroeconomic context for a well-organized effort by representatives of the American
business community not only to roll back the regulatory gains of the
public interest–labor coalition but to achieve tax relief as well.

That corporate attack was focused on such specific governmental
agencies as the Federal Trade Commission and the Occupational
Safety and Health Administration. The FTC, led by its activist chairman, Michael Pertschuk, was seeking to break new ground by ad-
vancing regulations to cover such matters as television advertising
directed at children. But such a proposed scrutiny of that medium
soon sparked strong opposition, which was captured by the *Washington Post*'s derisive remark that the FTC was fast becoming America's
"National Nanny." This sarcasm reflected well the fact that in ideological terms Ralph Nader had now been superseded by Irving Kristol
not only in the halls of Congress but across the country as well.

Trilateral Commission

That ideological shift was supported by business, which played its part by promoting antiregulatory advertising, as well as by its ample funding of conservative think tanks. Meanwhile, many voters on the grass-roots level were concerned that the American economy was in trouble; they now thought that it was time to deregulate in order to cut costs. Worried, then, about their job prospects at a time of obvious corporate difficulties, they made it clear to their representatives in Washington that they no longer supported the regulatory policies of the early seventies. And their stance, in turn, affected how Congress voted on various regulatory measures after 1977.

While middle-class voters pondered their future, corporate America established a powerful lobbying presence in Washington to advance its agenda, which included not only antiregulatory goals but tax cuts as well. Literally thousands of lobbyists came to town to work on behalf of that agenda for Fortune 500 companies, the Chamber of Commerce, and the National Federation of Independent Business. In addition, Washington, in the seventies, became the major headquarters of such leading national business organizations as the National Association of Manufacturers. At the same time, the Business Roundtable, while often meeting with President Carter, busily coordinated its policies with other organizations in order to achieve a consensus on matters important to American business. Given that unity of purpose, corporate America's active campaign for a reduction in the capital gains tax and corporate tax rates soon met with success following the vote on Proposition 13. Congress, moving with the political tide, embraced the conservative argument on behalf of supply-side economics, indicating that the era of liberal reform that began in the Kennedy-Johnson years was now over.

In addition, the emergence of the political action committee (PAC) helped to produce a positive outcome for corporate lobbyists. As a result of the 1974 Federal Elections Act and the Supreme Court decision in *Buckley v. Valeo*, the door had been opened for increased corporate involvement in national politics, which boosted the fortunes of the Republican party. The growth of business investment in politics can be measured by the following data: in 1974, Labor PACs numbered 201, business 89; in 1976, business PACs increased to 433, labor to 224; in 1978, business PACs jumped to 784; and in July 1980, they reached 1204. In actual dollar terms, corporate and trade PACs gave $10.7 million in 1976, $9.8 million in 1978, and $19.2 million in 1980, amounts that far exceeded what labor could either give or match. And since money talks in America, influence was purchased at a time when many legislators already used expensive television advertising as the most suitable medium for organizing and sustaining their political campaigns.

In 1976, corporations spent their money about equally between Democrats and Republicans, a practice that later drew Ronald Reagan's condemnation. By 1978, however, large and small business, now united as a class in opposition to a liberal agenda in Congress, employed another approach: in order to push the ideological center of gravity to the right, it gave substantial sums to Republican challengers who were sympathetic to a business point of view. And a significant amount of that corporate money, which was donated to those PACs, came from the country's most powerful corporations. In 1978, for example, each firm in the top ten gave $70,000, while those near the bottom of the top 500 firms provided about $6,000 per firm. Thanks to that financial input, which helped to reinforce an already active grass-roots business mobilization, corporate America was able to block labor law reform, the creation of a consumer protection agency, the passage of common situs legislation, and the enforcement of the rules and regulations issued by the FTC and OSHA.

While Republican party candidates benefited from such sizable corporate contributions, the party itself was also aided by contributions from people who responded to its direct mail drives of the late seventies. Building on the successful tactics employed by the environmental and consumer movements and later refined by Richard Viguerie and the New Right, the Republican party had become adept in finding the financial resources it needed to survive in the television age. In 1977–78, the Republican National Committee, the Republican Senate Campaign Committee, and the Republican Congressional Campaign Committee received $84.5 million, as compared to the $25.4 million given to equivalent Democratic committees. In 1979–80, those same Republican committees had been given $169.5 million, while their Democratic counterparts took in a paltry $37.2 million, representing a mere 21.9 percent of the dollars that the GOP had obtained during that same period.

The GOP's access to such a vast amount of money was only part of the story of its revival in the post-Watergate era. The party also placed great emphasis on tracking polls, focus groups, census data, and consulting firms in order to take advantage of that vast disparity in funding, which now separated it from the national Democratic party. Moreover, the Republicans now had the issues of the day working in their favor, which was far more important than its mastery of the new political technology. Adverse public reaction to the administration's handling of such contentious domestic issues as inflation, unemployment, taxes, energy, prayer in the public schools, and abortion went far to advance and to promote the political prospects of the Republican party. In addition, Jimmy Carter's inability to free the hostages taken from the American Embassy in Teheran increased the level of frustration inside the body politic, which in time worked against him and for the Republicans.

Despite the GOP comeback, there was little evidence to indicate that a majority of Americans either favored or wanted a right-wing policy agenda. On the contrary, poll data confirmed, in 1979–80, that a strong public commitment to the welfare state remained in place and that governmental services were viewed by the electorate as a positive good, as long as those services were provided in a cost-efficient manner. According to a *Washington Post* poll, voters were willing to pay taxes even for welfare programs, wanting only the abusers of that system to be denied benefits. On the other hand, the question of high taxes indeed rankled many people, whose mistrust of the government was so intense that they felt that taxes had to be cut in order to force it to operate in a more businesslike way. Thus, at a time when stagflation had seemingly become a way of life for everyone, more and more Americans now desired both a fairer system of taxation and, above all, an end to the alleged bureaucratic waste and sloth in Washington. Given those feelings, they were prepared to listen to politicians who promised them relief at both ends of their tax dollar.

While many voters lost confidence in the Democrats' ability to manage the economy, conservative Republicans found unity within diversity. Despite their often real differences over policy matters and ideology, they came together to support the Kemp-Roth Bill, which called for a 30 percent reduction in taxes over a three-year period, and they endorsed a rapid buildup of American strategic forces to cope with a real or alleged Soviet superiority in nuclear weaponry.

That convergence in views also dovetailed with the massive retailing of a conservative ideological perspective on both domestic and foreign policy matters. Conservative think tanks and journals, funded by such wealthy sponsors as William Simon of the Olin Foundation, provided the populace with a coherent prescription for revitalizing the American economy along the lines of a tax cut and deregulation of the economy. The Committee on the Present Danger, an elitist advocacy group led by Paul Nitze, offered a harsh critique of Carter's efforts to negotiate a strategic arms limitation agreement with Moscow. And in each case, the Carter administration found it difficult to offer either an effective policy rebuttal or to stanch its loss of support inside the country. This, then, was the context for the 1980 presidential election campaign, which pitted Carter, an unpersuasive defender of the status quo, against a crusading and surging conservatism, whose leading spokesman, Ronald Reagan, promised the American people a change in leadership and direction.

Heading into 1980, Carter's first serious challenge came from Senator Edward Kennedy, who sought to mobilize liberal forces inside the Democratic party to support his bid for the party's nomination; his effort, however, was soon undercut by a development that had a significant role in determining the ultimate outcome of the 1980 election. The Iranian hostage crisis gave Carter an opportunity to utilize a Rose Garden strategy, allowing him to avoid a debate with Kennedy over such matters as price and wage controls. And after Kennedy failed to win the important Illinois primary, Carter virtually locked up the party's nomination.

Yet having won that fight, Carter still could not overcome the consequences of stagflation, even as he moved steadily away from the traditional welfare state agenda of his party. By 1980, then, rampant inflation, combined with the further globalization of the American economy, a growing tax revolt, the spread of urban disorder, and severe cultural conflict among the Democratic party's many constituencies, had left him without adequate political and ideological resources to defend the party's traditional commitments to the Keynesian welfare state.

Meanwhile, Republicans, galvanized by Carter's manifold troubles, went about their business of selecting a ticket and drafting a platform for the campaign to come. Among the candidates seeking the party's presidential nomination were Ronald Reagan, George Bush, John Connally, and Congressman John Anderson. Interestingly, Richard Viguerie favored Connally, the former Texas governor and Nixon cabinet member, who he thought was suitably seasoned and committed to support a right-wing policy agenda in the event he made it to the White House. Many corporate executives, given their concern about Reagan's lack of experience and his endorsement of the Kemp-Roth Bill, backed either Connally or George Bush. Fearful that the proposed tax cut would increase the budget deficit, they worried that such a deficit would make it more difficult to lower corporate taxes.

But Connally lacked the broad personal appeal and political base necessary to do well in the Republican primaries; few conservative voters could readily support a candidate who had been so closely associated with both Lyndon Johnson and Richard Nixon. Reagan had no such problem; his credentials and past record indicated unswerving loyalty and service to conservative causes and beliefs. From his days as governor of California to his recent opposition to the Panama Canal treaties, Reagan had been the most outspoken and best-known figure of rightist views inside the Republican party. And his popularity among most conservatives inside the GOP had never been in doubt. Not only had he been the candidate of choice among many conservative delegates to the 1968 Republican convention, but he had just missed taking the nomination away from President Gerald Ford in 1976. Now, in 1980, Reagan's momentum made him the front runner at a time when the political center of gravity inside the Republican party had moved rapidly to the right ideologically and to the Sunbelt geographically.

Congressman John Anderson's failure to win much support for his own candidacy underscored the collapse of the once-dominant liberal wing of the GOP. The current Republican whip in the House, Anderson's libertarian social views on such matters as abortion and the Equal Rights Amendment outraged the conservative bloc, which now played such an important and decisive role in so many Republican primaries. Yet the votes that Anderson received in a number of key New England primaries, which might otherwise have gone to George Bush, hurt Bush's effort to mount a more effective challenge to Reagan across the country. With the support of Sunbelt votes and money, Reagan soon dispatched Bush and other competitors, allowing him to head into Detroit, the site of the 1980 Republican convention, with the nomination in his pocket.

The Republican convention was a triumph for those elements in the party who saw in Reagan the true and authentic spokesman for their various conservative causes and goals. His broad appeal was such that the Reverend Jerry Falwell, the major organizer of the Moral Majority; Norman Podhoretz, a leading advocate of a neoconservative foreign and domestic policy; Jack Kemp, supply-sider par excellence; and William Buckley, editor of the *National Review*, each favored his nomination. Most Republicans agreed with Buckley that Reagan's selection of George Bush as his running mate was a "logical choice." In fact, it was a shrewd move that Buckley himself had recommended several months earlier to Reagan's staff in order to limit possible defections from moderate and liberal Republicans to John Anderson, now running as an independent candidate for the presidency.

The Republican platform writers touched base with those key interest groups and constituencies forming the nucleus of the Reagan coalition. Those who opposed abortion and the ERA, wanted prayer restored to the public schools, supported tax cuts and deregulation of the American economy, endorsed a strengthened military, and desired a more aggressive American foreign policy had their views incorporated into that platform. Such was the conservative agenda, originating in the right-wing politics and ideology of the fifties and sixties, that Ronald Reagan would offer the American people in 1980.

In the meantime, the Democrats had their own convention business to address. They met in New York and renominated Jimmy Carter and Walter Mondale just a few short weeks after Carter had slumped to 21 percent in the Gallup Poll, which was the lowest approval rating it ever recorded for a sitting president. Desperate for support, Carter went along with a party platform that recapitulated the goals and accomplishments of Democratic party liberalism in order to appeal to traditional Democratic constituencies he now so desperately needed. Ironically, he now sought to identify himself both at the convention and later in the campaign with Kennedy-style liberalism, which was not in keeping with his real views and policies.

Carter, in practice, was also the politician of limits, whose programmatic shift to the right on fiscal and social policy was an attempt to come to terms with the now-prevailing wisdom that federal budget deficits, not OPEC price hikes and rising food prices, were chiefly responsible for producing the mounting inflation of the day. So despite his rhetorical commitment to the legacy of a government of good deeds and social compassion, both he and his party, in the summer of 1980, were committed to the politics and goals of a balanced budget and fiscal restraints. By repudiating the principle that managed deficits had a significant role to play in protecting the welfare state, Carter and most congressional Democrats sacrificed a longstanding party commitment to a fiscal policy that had distinguished them in recent years from the Republican party. Because they could not provide an alternative intellectual and political framework to cope with the harsh reality of 7 percent unemployment and 12.4 percent inflation in an election year, the Democrats conceded to Ronald Reagan the argument that big government deficits and a gigantic federal bureaucracy were responsible for the country's economic woes.

Even worse, the Carter administration, with the help of Federal Reserve Board chairman Paul Volcker, produced a political business cycle that resulted in negative economic growth in 1980. Earlier in the year, they had worked together to induce a recession in an attempt to bring down inflation. And their accomplishment was such that during the second quarter, as journalist William Greider points out, "the GNP shrank by $39 billion dollars in real terms, adjusted for inflation. . . . Industrial production decreased by more than 8 percent. Unemployment jumped from 6.3 percent in March to 7.8 percent by July. . . . [And] real per capita income dropped from $4,503 to $4,435."

When Volcker increased the money supply in the spring of 1980, the economy began to grow at a rate of 2.4 percent in the third quarter, as compared to a drop of nearly 10 percent in the second quarter. But just weeks before the election, he again raised interest rates to cope with rising inflation. That action, taken against the wishes of the White House, produced a sudden sharp economic downturn that could not have come at a more inopportune time for Carter; it left him to face the electorate with a economic record that was far worse than any president had offered the country in an election year since Herbert Hoover in 1932. Unfortunately for Carter, voters could not remember that during his first three years in office there had been reasonable growth and that the unemployment rate had dropped by several percentage points. But because they are far more responsive to their current situation than to past experiences, especially in an election year, Carter was caught in an economic vise largely of his own making from which there was no escape.

The crisis confronting Carter at home and abroad was ready made for Ronald Reagan, who had been on the attack long before the outset of the fall campaign. For years he had blamed "liberalism" for hamstringing the American economy, arguing that big government and high taxes were preventing the market from doing its job of providing increased opportunities for employment and profits. At a time when stagflation and the globalization of the American economy had converged to undermine the prospect of stable economic growth and to reduce living standards for American workers, Reagan offered worried voters, in the words of economist Herbert Stein, the "economics of joy." He repudiated traditional Republican economic doctrine, which was predicated on tight fiscal policy and the quest for balanced budgets, and, instead, proposed that taxes be cut, military spending be increased, and a deficit be incurred all at the same time.

A recent convert to supply-side economics, Reagan now believed that by stimulating economic growth through a tax cut, governmental revenues, resulting from the business boom to come, would be sufficiently enhanced to bring the budget back into balance in the near future. During the primary campaign, George Bush had labeled Reagan's proposed strategy for dealing with an ailing American economy as "voodoo economics." John Anderson called it an exercise in "blue smoke and mirrors." But most Reagan supporters, including Jack Kemp, believed that a tax cut was the sine qua non for getting the American economy back on its feet. For them the ideology of the "free lunch," which was implicit in their economic approach, was the best possible answer to Jimmy Carter's argument for limits and a call for sacrifice from the American people.

Reagan also mounted a relentless attack on Carter's foreign policy. Pointing to the Russian invasion of Afghanistan and the continuing captivity of the American hostages in Teheran, he tapped into a deep well of frustration and anxiety in the country. A majority of Americans were worried, too, about the current state of Soviet-American relations, and they now believed that the Soviet Union was seeking, or had already achieved, superiority over the United States in the area of strategic nuclear delivery systems. Hence, they endorsed Reagan's demand for a major buildup of America's military capability in order to counter a real or alleged Soviet threat.

Reagan's views on these matters were virtually identical to the strategic perspective offered by the Committee on the Present Danger, which he joined in 1979. That organization had opposed Jimmy Carter's efforts to obtain an arms control agreement with the Soviets, arguing that any such agreement would compromise the national security of the United States by leaving the Soviets with their military superiority intact. Later, many Democrats associated with the CPD, including Paul Nitze, the organization's cofounder, and Jeane J. Kirkpatrick, a political scientist at Georgetown University, publicly endorsed Reagan's bid for the White House. They felt that Carter was simply too weak and irresolute to do the job of confronting the Soviets. They supported Reagan despite the fact that Carter, after 1978, had moved to the right on national security issues by adding billions to the military budget, denouncing the Soviet invasion of Afghanistan, and refusing to allow the United States to participate in the 1980 summer Olympic Games in Moscow or to export wheat to the Soviet Union.

While Reagan picked up solid political support for his foreign policy views from an important bloc of neoconservative Democrats, he also continued to appeal to those right-wing elements that had helped nominate him in Detroit. He sided with the Moral Majority on such issues as abortion and prayer in the public schools and encouraged the Reverend Jerry Falwell and others of similar persuasion to continue their work of registering new voters on his behalf. In addition, Reagan won the support of the moguls of corporate America by endorsing a tax cut for the corporations and supporting a federal bailout for the Chrysler Corporation. These moves gave members of the Business Roundtable the assurances that they needed to oppose Jimmy Carter, since his record lacked the consistency and the active support that business was looking for. In 1980, then, corporate PACs were heavily weighted on the side of the GOP, as business expected action and deeds, not merely good intentions, from Reagan and the Republicans.

By the same token, Reagan also found considerable support from many blue-collar workers inside the American labor movement. His easy, friendly, telegenic style appealed to them in such places as Youngstown, Ohio. As elsewhere, they got the message that he was prepared to stand up for America abroad and not pander to blacks at home. Thus, at a time when their own living standards were declining, blue-collar Americans were very receptive to Reagan's argument that it was necessary "to get the government off our backs." They probably believed that any move to deregulate the activities of the federal government was also a move against forced busing and affirmative action programs.

In the course of his campaign, Reagan shrewdly managed to turn blue- collar/populist resentment away from the corporate system and focused it instead on big government and the welfare state. He also strongly endorsed traditional American values of hard work, upward mobility, and individual achievement, not a system of support that provided benefits for "welfare queens." Reagan's use of such rhetoric was a clear indication that he and his advisers understood well the point that Kevin Phillips had made in *The Emerging Republican Majority:* "The principal force which broke up the Democratic [New Deal] coalition is the Negro socio-economic revolution and the liberal Democratic ideological inability to cope with it. . . . The Democratic Party fell victim to the ideological impetus of a liberalism which had carried it beyond programs taxing the few for the benefit of the many [the New Deal] to programs taxing the many on behalf of the few [the Great Society]."

More specifically, the intense hostility that many white voters felt for affirmative action programs, coupled with their desire to reduce spending on welfare and public housing, had given conservative Republicans an opportunity to employ wedge tactics for the purpose of splitting the largely class-based Democratic coalition along racial lines. Using racial codes to mobilize whites on behalf of a conservative populism, Republicans like Senator Jesse Helms of North Carolina had achieved political success because they were able to identify the liberal establishment with black causes and cultural radicalism. It was a tactical lesson that other Republicans would not soon forget or ignore.

If race had become a winning issue for the GOP, so to a lesser degree did gender issues and conflicts. Millions of women did not share the enthusiasm of left-liberals for the ERA, or necessarily aspire to a career in the market economy. Committed to "family values," they embraced a moral traditionalism predicated, in part, on opposition to both gay rights and abortion. Like conservative men, they were ready to vote for Reagan because his position on social issues also spoke to their concern about the spread of pornography, as well as a concomitant fear that the public education system was controlled by "secular humanists."

As sociologist Rebecca Klatch shows in her *Women of the New Right,* class and religious involvement played a very significant role in determining the choices women made with respect to their political and social views. Those who were poorly educated homemakers, possessing strong or intense religious commitments, most often supported a conservative political and social agenda. Those who were better educated, career-oriented, and secular in their outlook generally endorsed ERA and other causes associated with a liberal feminist social agenda. Based on Klatch's research, it is clear that one source of conservative strength, then, was a fusion of interests between those tied to a fundamentalist world-view and those interested in putting a conservative establishment in power.

Years earlier, George Wallace had revealed the racial fault line inside the national Democratic party, which the GOP then exploited. Richard Nixon and Spiro Agnew soon found the Silent Majority, which gave them their opportunity to denounce those in the counterculture who trashed national symbols like the American flag or mocked family values. Although Reagan benefited from those earlier tactics and approaches, his political mobilization was somewhat different in that he combined a more direct emphasis on social issues and racial politics with an economic agenda tied specifically to tax cuts, regulatory rollbacks, and a reduction in the size and scope of the federal government. While Nixon worked within a welfare state framework, Reagan was the spokesman for a dynamic conservative movement, which demanded major changes in the liberal status quo.

Yet Reagan's close connection with that movement worried many voters across the country, concerned as they were about his reputation for taking extremist positions on foreign and domestic matters. Reagan tried to reassure them by announcing during the campaign that he would pursue arms control talks with the Soviet Union, and, furthermore, he would respect the integrity and the inviolability of the Social Security system. He and his advisers understood well the need for moderation in the pursuit of votes in order to avoid the outlandish political mistakes that Barry Goldwater had made in his campaign of 1964.

That point was brought home dramatically in the course of the television debate between Carter and Reagan, which took place in Cleveland ten days before the election and at a time when the two candidates, according to the polls, were locked in a virtual dead heat. Reagan—despite his reputation for holding hard-line views—appeared so personally unthreatening and moderate in tone that the horns that Carter tried to put on him were not visible to most viewers in the television audience. Reagan, on the other hand, delivered a body blow to Carter by asking those same viewers how many of them were now better off than they had been four years ago. Because they were trying to cope with high interest rates, growing unemployment, continuing inflation, and a steady loss of purchasing power, Reagan's question convinced many of those who still remained undecided that it was now time for a change.

Although Reagan won only 50.7 percent of the popular vote, he scored a landslide victory in the electoral college, doing particularly well in an area that was now a major source of Republican strength, the Sunbelt and the Rocky Mountain West. In the face of the Reagan rout, Carter received 41 percent of the popular vote and carried only a few states, including his home state of Georgia. John Anderson, running as an independent, won only 7 percent of the vote (mostly from upper-middle-class social libertarians) and carried no states, but he may have denied Carter a state here and there where the margins separating the two major candidates were fairly close.

The Republicans also captured the Senate for the first time since 1952, which, as it turned out, was a very important complement to Reagan's own success. By winning twelve new seats in what was the biggest turnover in many years, they managed to defeat such liberal Democratic stalwarts as George McGovern, Frank Church, Birch Bayh, and John Culver. The party also added thirty-three new members to its depleted ranks in the House, making it easier for a future Reagan White House to deal with that chamber. All in all, the election of 1980 was a smashing triumph for the conservative movement, which had brought Reagan to power after having existed for so many years in the wilderness of American politics.

A majority of those who voted for Reagan and against Carter clearly wanted change. Fed up with Carter's domestic and foreign policies, they took a chance on Reagan even though they did not support his domestic agenda or even find him a particularly attractive candidate. Poll data, in fact, showed that although Carter was the most unpopular president since the end of World War II, Reagan was the least popular candidate to capture the White House in the same period. Despite that feeling, Reagan won by majorities in all regions of the country, which strongly suggests that his victory was no accident but the result of complex forces that converged at the same time to help put him in the White House.

The combination of persistent inflation and higher marginal tax rates for the middle and lower middle classes had made many people susceptible to Reagan's claim that inflation had been produced by huge and unnecessary federal deficits. He cleverly put the onus for those deficits on the back of the welfare state, claiming that it was responsible for draining important resources away from productive investment in the private economy. Reagan also offered his supply-side prescriptions for restoring growth, which appeared to many to be the right approach at the right time. In addition, Reagan played on the anger and frustration of the American people, who were outraged by the Iranian takeover of the American embassy in Teheran and were also fearful that the Soviets had pulled ahead in the arms race. He promised the country that if he became president, American pride, power, and position would be restored internationally.

At the time Reagan delivered his message, the national Democratic party was in shambles. Because the party was poorly financed, intellectually impoverished, and internally polarized as a result of intense racial and ethnic conflict, it lacked the necessary resources to take on the spirited challenge offered by a well-financed, confident conservative movement. In addition, the unraveling of the party system, which political scientist Walter Dean Burnham saw in the making in the late sixties, had played havoc with the traditional Democratic base around the country. With the declining political importance of urban America and organized labor, voters no longer had the same partisan loyalties of an earlier period. And with fewer Democrats around, and even fewer bothering to vote for the presidential ticket, the task of the Republican party was made that much easier. In the meantime, the GOP was winning the votes of affluent suburbanites in the rapidly emerging demographic heartland of American politics because it promised them the prospect of lower taxes and less governmental regulation.

The process of political change was most evident in the South, where, unlike the rest of the country, a political realignment had left that region firmly in the hands of the presidential Republican party. Also, conservative Republican senators were elected that year from Florida, Alabama, Georgia, and North Carolina, helped significantly with votes and support provided by the New Religious Right. Although many liberals greatly exaggerated its national political importance, the New Religious Right had become a significant force inside the Republican party, by playing an important role organizing voter registration drives. Those who voted for Reagan and other conservatives because of Jerry Falwell's efforts surely left their mark on the politics of the region.

The estimated $25 million dollars that right-wing oil entrepreneurs from Texas, Oklahoma, and Louisiana gave to the GOP to elect conservative Republicans to Congress was also important in advancing Republican prospects in 1980. With that kind of money at their disposal, it is no mystery why many GOP candidates won in 1980. Longtime Senate liberals such as Gaylord Nelson and Frank Church, lacking a competitive financial base to defend their political turf from right-wing challengers, were vulnerable to well-organized, financially secure campaigns, which thrived in the conservative political climate that prevailed in 1980. Yet Senate liberals often ran well ahead of Carter, suggesting that his presence at the top of the ticket damaged their chances to win reelection. In fact, eight of the twelve Republicans newly elected to the Senate carried their respective states that year by a margin of less than 2 percent.

Corporate America, like Sunbelt oil barons, played a major role in financing a Republican victory in 1980. Because it wanted a changed political environment in Washington, business gave generously to the Republican candidates, contributing $19.2 million to PACs in order to defeat as many liberal Democratic incumbents as possible. Nearly one-third of all funds collected by corporate PACs that year were funneled to the conservative Republican challengers. On the other hand, Republican incumbents received twenty times more money from business than business gave to Democratic challengers. And where the race was close, business support always went to the Republicans.

Business had invested wisely and well, given the election returns. According to the *New York Times*, business insiders—the day after the election—were confident "that the president-elect would oversee the most probusiness administration since that of Dwight D. Eisenhower." And Reginald Jones, chairman of the Business Roundtable, thought that the conservative victory "should provide considerable encouragement for the private sector, resulting in increased economic activity." That business was to be a major beneficiary of the Reagan victory was not in question. Corporate tax cuts would surely be forthcoming as promised by Reagan during the campaign, and a different regulatory climate would be created as well. Whether such steps, taken by themselves, would be sufficient to create a more favorable domestic and international environment for American business was another matter.

Interestingly, just after Reagan became president, a new regime took power in France as a result of widespread voter dissatisfaction with the way a centrist-right government had managed the economy. With the election of François Mitterrand as president of France, and a Social Democratic majority in the National Assembly, France would seek to move in a different economic direction from where the Reagan administration was headed. But despite their very significant programmatic differences, these heads of state still had something in common: they each took power because their predecessor, whether Jimmy Carter or Valéry Giscard d'Estaing, could not find an adequate solution to the omnipresent problem of stagflation. Mounting criticism of their respective governments' economic performance by intellectuals and policy analysts (the one on the left, the other on the right) helped to bring about a shift in the climate of opinion that led to a political change in each country. But even before Mitterrand took power, it was already clear in the United States that Reagan's victory had delivered a body blow to political liberalism, leaving it in a state of near collapse throughout the country.

5

The Reagan Revolution

When Ronald Reagan became president of the United States at noon on January 20, 1981, he brought to the office a conservative world-view. This had not always been his position. A fervent admirer of Franklin Roosevelt, for whom he voted four times, Reagan had also supported Harry Truman in 1948. But in the aftermath of his unhappy experiences with Communists who were active in the Hollywood labor movement during and after World War II, he began a gradual move to the right, at a time when the cold war had become the dominant political reality of life at home and abroad. Once he had forsaken the earnest liberalism of his past, Reagan voted for Dwight Eisenhower in 1952, marking his shift from a liberal Democrat to an ideological conservative, a transition that his marriage in 1951 to the politically conservative Nancy Davis did much to encourage.

In the fifties, Reagan left Hollywood to work for the General Electric Company, giving speeches to company employees and others about the virtues and benefits of the free enterprise system and the American way. In addition, he functioned as the genial host of television's General Electric Theater, where his polished manner and poise served him well in this new and increasingly important medium of popular entertainment and culture. In the early sixties, Reagan formally changed his political registration in California from Democrat to Republican. He made this change just as his pronounced right-wing views were beginning to attract the attention of well-placed, wealthy figures of the Republican right such as oil magnate Henry Salvatori, the "Godfather" of southern California conservatism.

After Barry Goldwater's failed presidential bid in 1964, Salvatori and other self-made millionaires such as Holmes Tuttle saw in Reagan a fresh opportunity to advance their antilabor, antistatist, and probusiness views. Thanks to their prompting and strong financial support, he made a nationally televised speech in support of Goldwater just before the 1964 election. That speech served as his political debut; not only did it allow Reagan to spell out a conservative policy agenda for the future, but it also gave him the opportunity to promote the ideology of the right in the smooth, self-assured manner that would become his hallmark for television viewers in the years and decades to come. He called for a worldwide crusade against communism, vastly lower taxes, and a major reduction in the size and scope of the federal government. By recapitulating the major themes of sixties conservatism in such a compelling way, his speech quickly gained the respect and admiration of many people originally attracted to the Goldwater movement.

Encouraged and bankrolled by the same people who sponsored his nationally televised address on the eve of the 1964 election, Reagan entered the race for governor of California in 1966. After winning the primary battle against George Christopher, a moderate, mainstream Republican, he challenged incumbent governor Edmund "Pat" Brown in the fall election. Although Brown had scored a resounding victory over Richard Nixon in 1962, he was in some political difficulty in 1966. Nevertheless, he clearly underestimated the political skill and personal appeal of his opponent. And why not? Brown, after all, was an able governor of a state whose public infrastructure, in the form of primary and secondary schools, state universities, and highways was arguably the best to be found anywhere in the country. In his mind, Reagan was a former movie actor, a mere Hollywood celebrity, whose political views had already been repudiated nationally as a result of Lyndon Johnson's landslide victory over Goldwater in 1964.

Reagan defeated Brown by nearly a million votes in November, even though the California economy was humming and its fabled lifestyle still very much intact. The California election, as well as others in the country, revealed all too clearly that the national Democratic party, only two years after its great victory of 1964, was already in deep trouble with the electorate; for 1966 was the year when the white backlash became a reality for many voters across the country. Disgusted with the riots in Watts and elsewhere, fed up with growing campus disorder, outraged by the flag- and draft card-burning antics of individuals in the antiwar movement, they expressed their anger by supporting Republican candidates for state and national office who were perceived to be on the side of law and order and against permissiveness and programs for the poor.

The situation that year was ready-made for Reagan, who capitalized on his opportunity by telling voters that he strongly opposed the campus protests on the Berkeley campus of the University of California; by the same token, he implicitly conveyed a similar message about the Watts riot in the summer of 1965. While appearing in the course of the campaign as the vigilant spokesman for law and order and defender of traditional values, Reagan sought to hold Brown responsible for the recent happenings at Berkeley and other untoward events elsewhere in the state. His message, which was delivered with great telegenic style, so coincided with the voters' mood that he was elected to serve two consecutive four-year terms as governor from 1967 to 1975.

Reagan's eight years in Sacramento prefigured what was to come when he later went to Washington. His was a businessman's government, administered by people who were committed to the ideology of free markets and the politics of laissez faire. Not surprisingly, then, Holmes Tuttle, a close friend and key adviser to Reagan on personnel matters, imposed an ideological litmus test on appointments to positions in state government. As one of the new men of power who had earlier pushed Reagan to the fore, he made certain that "liberals" were not hired by a governor who wanted, above all, to reduce the role and trim the functions of government.

Reagan's obsession with tax cuts went back to the days when he and others like him in Hollywood made the kind of money that placed them in the highest tax bracket. Although very few Americans of his generation ever earned enough income in a given year to be taxed at the 82 percent to 91 percent marginal rate, Reagan, years after his movie career had ended, remained bitter at the memory of what he considered to be a tax-gouging enterprise carried on by the federal government during his most productive years at Warner Brothers and other studios. Ironically, though, while confronting a growing deficit that he inherited from his predecessor, Reagan signed legislation raising state taxes. Nevertheless, when the tax revolt of the late seventies finally surfaced in the form of Proposition 13, he had no problem siding rhetorically with the tax cutters.

The other theme that obsessed Reagan as governor was the size and scope of government. Very much in the Calvin Coolidge tradition, he earnestly believed that government was not the solution for whatever ailed America. Reagan saw government as a obstacle to personal achievement and opportunity because he so strongly identified with the tradition of the self-reliant and self-made individual, which also characterized the ideology and outlook of his closest political supporters. A product of the American heartland, as well as of a celebrity-minded Los Angeles culture, he felt that others could also do well with hard work and imagination in a country such as the United States where careers were wide open to talent.

On the more mundane level of politics, however, Reagan did not always get everything he wanted in the state capital. He had to work with such astute Democrats as Jesse Unruh and Bob Moretti, the key figures in the California Assembly. Forced to compromise, Reagan made deals with them in order to get at least part of his program through the Democrat-controlled legislature. More of a political realist than many of his more avid supporters, he played the game without changing his larger views as to what constituted good public policy, such as the need to contain governmental spending and to reduce the power of government. By moving from the modified Hamiltonianism of his New Deal days to a brand of Jeffersonianism, which was the hallmark of such conservative libertarians as Albert Jay Nock in the twenties and Friedrich Hayek in the forties and fifties, he had clearly identified himself with the antistatist tradition that went back to the earliest days of the Republic.

Yet Reagan not only had raised taxes during his eight years as governor but also had increased the state deficit from four billion to over ten billion dollars. In addition, he had protected the University of California from attacks from both left and right, and he had gone along with a major reform of the welfare system that authorized increased state aid for those most in need of public help. With all that behind him, Reagan still managed, as historian Garry Wills has shown, to convince himself—and perhaps his constituents as well— that he had lowered taxes and reduced governmental activity. Such was the mystery of his modus operandi that he was able to transcend the sharp contradiction between his public rhetoric and his political action without suffering serious damage to his personal image or his political standing with voters, especially on the Republican right.

Reagan's success stemmed from the fact that most Americans were like him on one level. That is, they generally distrusted government, supported a diffusion of power via their federalist system, feared the concentration of authority in Washington, believed in the virtues of the market economy, and embraced the values of an acquisitive society. Yet those same Americans, as poll data had repeatedly shown, wanted to keep intact specific welfare programs, including Social Security and Medicare; and they willingly took from the federal treasury an entire range of benefits and assistance on which the economic health of their communities and regions depended. In practice, then, they generally endorsed the politics and practice of the welfare state. And so did Reagan, who as governor of California had supported the mixed system of public-private support that had contributed to the enormous growth and power of that rapidly emerging superstate.

In Washington, Reagan had to cope with different problems than he did in Sacramento. As the leader of a conservative coalition that favored an increase in military spending, a rollback of Soviet power, the lowering of taxes, a reduction in welfare state programs and services, the deregulation of the economy, and opposition to abortion, he was in no mood to adhere to the status quo. In the context of domestic issues, he was prepared to replace the once dominant liberal consensus, predicated on the Keynesian welfare state, with one of his own making, consistent with the views he outlined on a variety of issues before and during the 1980 campaign. Eager to implement his agenda, Reagan looked to the future with hope and confidence. And like his hero Franklin Roosevelt, he categorically rejected the argument that America was either facing imminent decline or that it no longer was in complete command of its own destiny.

Reagan's triumph in 1980 ushered in a new era in American politics and life, giving confident conservatives a unique opportunity to offer their programmatic alternatives to the largely discredited liberalism of the seventies. While Reagan supplied the uplifting rhetoric and vision, others in his administration, coming from conservative think tanks, provided the necessary details and approach for dealing with the most pressing matter on the domestic agenda, the state of the American economy. They soon crafted a program that went far to incorporate the supply-side argument for corporate and personal tax cuts, which was also consistent with the objectives sought by such influential business lobbyists as Charls Walker and the powerful business coalition he represented.

As the spirit of Calvin Coolidge swept across the land, the accumulation of wealth as a civic enterprise was defended by journalist George Gilder in his book *Wealth and Poverty*, a work that Ronald Reagan purportedly loved. Published in 1981, it stood as the summa theologica of the early Reagan years, celebrating, above all, the virtues of entrepreneurial wealth as the major catalyst for creating the moral foundation of the good society. Giving three cheers for capitalism, Gilder offered an updated version of trickle-down economics that fit in well with the dominant ideological consensus of the day, which had at its core the need to create a good climate in which business could operate. Although Gilder was, in the words of historian Michael Katz, "[m]ore a moralist than analyst" of social reality, he was influential for a time, providing administration conservatives not only with a malicious critique of Great Society programs but also with an intellectual justification for an unfettered capitalism that served their policy purposes well during Reagan's first term.

One such conservative was David Stockman, who was busily at work in the White House producing a budget that reflected the economic goals and priorities of the new administration. At one time a student radical at Michigan State and later a divinity student at Harvard, Stockman also served for a time in the House of Representatives, where he made friends with fellow Republican Jack Kemp, that chamber's leading supply-sider. Because he possessed both talent and good connections, Stockman was brought into the Reagan administration to serve as its budget director. After producing a plan calling for substantial tax cuts and a reduction or elimination of funding for many Great Society programs, he hoped that his efforts would lead in the direction of a balanced budget in the near term. Given the military spending priorities of the Reagan White House and Congress's refusal or inability to make even deeper cuts in domestic programs that had already been sliced, the goal of a balanced budget was soon out of reach. Much to Stockman's subsequent dismay, he discovered that ideology and politics were operating at cross-purposes in the Reagan administration, sufficient to undermine his efforts to reduce the deficit.

A key element in the unfolding story of that growing budget deficit was the military buildup that President Reagan and Secretary of Defense Caspar Weinberger undertook in order to project massive American military power across the globe. They pushed the Carter administration's already augmented military budget to an even higher level, planning to spend $1.6 trillion over the next five fiscal years, as compared to Carter's projected $1.2 trillion for the same period. Although this move was initially supported by all elements of the Reagan coalition, as well as by a majority of Americans, Democratic and Republican alike, it dovetailed with the deep tax cuts of 1981 that, in turn, produced an annual budget deficit of over $200 billion by 1983, much to the consternation of many in the business community.

Reagan was not going to be deterred by the desire of businessmen, including some in defense industries, to reduce military spending in order to bring down the deficit. His hard-line foreign policy vis-à-vis the Soviet Union meant that the military budget, in the words of Martin Anderson, was going "to drive fiscal policy, not the other way around." Thus, it was hardly an accident that a form of military Keynesianism came to dominate the budget deliberations virtually from the beginning of Reagan's first term. But as it later turned out, increased military spending, coupled with the tax cut of 1981, helped to produce the staggering debt load that the country would have to carry into the nineties.

That tax cut was at the top of Reagan's domestic legislative agenda. Along with the military buildup, it was the common denominator that united the various elements of his coalition and a key to his program of producing economic growth and abundance at home. A firm believer in its curative powers, Reagan pushed hard for congressional action throughout the spring and summer of 1981. While House Speaker Thomas O'Neill tried to mobilize his forces to resist Reagan's initiative, they were effectively muzzled by an outpouring of public sympathy extended to him following the attempt on his life in late March 1981. Although very few people realized how close the president came to dying in the immediate aftermath of the shooting, and few knew that his recovery was taking longer and turning out to be more difficult and prolonged than the White House ever revealed, the event itself clearly bonded Reagan with the American people, who now gave him the popular grass-roots support he needed to pressure Congress to pass his program.

There were a number of other elements that went into the making of Reagan's consensus. Reagan's call for tax cuts hit home for millions of citizens who had suffered a serious erosion in purchasing power resulting from persistent inflation, which, among other consequences, had placed them in higher tax brackets. So the argument that a readjustment in tax rates would benefit them made good sense to many Americans during a period of declining living standards. At the same time, corporate America felt that it, too, was entitled to tax relief and other benefits in order to compete more effectively in the now-globalized market place. Consequently, the supply side argument carried the day, with corporate spokesmen arguing that a tax cut would serve as an incentive to spur fresh investment in productive facilities, while blue-collar and middle-class Americans hoped that it would reduce the pressure on their pocketbooks.

Thus, with the ideological and political foundations for a tax cut now firmly in place, the Reagan administration maneuvered a willing Congress to act in accord with David Stockman's design, which included a tax cut of roughly 25 percent spread over three years, as well as a significant reduction in federal spending for many domestic social programs. The fulfillment of a supply-sider's dream, the Economic Recovery Tax Act of 1981 (ERTA) served as the centerpiece of the Reagan administration's effort to stimulate growth and to produce new investment. But a large and important truth was concealed from the public at the time of the congressional debate over ERTA, which Stockman later revealed to journalist William Greider. As Stockman put it: "The point of the supply-side tax cut is dropping the top rate from 70 to 50 percent—the rest is a secondary matter. . . . In order to make this palatable as a political matter you had to bring down all brackets. . . . Kemp-Roth was always a Trojan Horse to bring down the top rate." He also kept from Congress (and perhaps from Reagan, too) his plan to use the huge deficit created by the tax cut to force Congress to make significant reductions in its spending on current social programs, and to prevent it from funding new welfare programs that Reaganites of his persuasion opposed on ideological grounds.

Since both the tax cut and the budget cut went to the heart of the Reagan Revolution, a more detailed look at each reveals something important about the ideas and interests that were mobilized on their behalf in Congress. From the perspective of supply-siders like Jude Wanniski and George Gilder, a tax cut for the rich would put fresh money into the hands of investors who would then have the wherewithal and means to make financial commitments on which future jobs and further investment opportunities depended. Their ideas— rooted in the economic theories of professors Robert Mundell and Arthur Laffer—produced a quick payoff following Ronald Reagan's victory in 1980, which was an ample reward indeed for those conservative think tanks and corporate interests that had earlier sponsored their work.

Although the Democratic leadership in the House of Representatives tried to alter and deflect Reagan's tax bill, it lacked the political and intellectual resources to mount an effective challenge. Some Democrats, led by Congressman Dan Rostenkowski, engaged in a bidding war with the administration in order to please business, a major source of campaign contributions. For example, independent oil producers, who had worked so hard to defeat liberal Democrats in 1980, were given tax breaks that the administration had not included in its original tax proposal; thanks to key Democratic support, other industries, too, received similar benefits. Helped by the prevailing mood of business-government cooperation in the House, the White House easily mustered the votes it needed to override all Democratic objections to its bill; the Senate, which was controlled by the GOP, posed no problem. After Congress completed its work on the measure, President Reagan signed ERTA into law on August 13, 1981. A major piece of legislation, it was destined to leave its mark on the budgetary process and fiscal policy for years to come.

As the administration intended, the chief beneficiaries of this supply-side windfall were wealthy Americans as well as the American business community, the major constituents of Reaganomics. In general terms, the 1981 tax act mandated that rates would be reduced over a three-year period by 25 percent, with the top rate coming down from 70 to 50 percent. Or to put it in more class-oriented terms, estate taxes were substantially reduced, and rates on unearned income and capital gains were also targeted for relief. As a result of such action, the income of the top 0.2 percent of all income filers had increased by 21 to 26 percent by 1984, whereas the gain in disposable income for those at the median point was a nominal 3.5 percent. Meanwhile, families under $10,000 lost more than 15 percent of their income due to various tax and budget changes enacted in 1981. Such, in general terms, were the economic and social results of the $750 billion cut that ERTA had projected and authorized over a three-year period.

Business, too, benefited from the tax legislation of 1981. Corporate taxes were substantially reduced, and individual sectors such as energy received special consideration from Congress resulting from the competition between Democrats and Republicans seeking the favor of business. In addition, business was aided by legislation designed to accelerate the rapid depreciation allowance, and investment tax credits were also included in the package that was drafted after much consultation with business lobbyists. All in all, a unified corporate America received a handsome reward, amounting to a $150 billion tax cut over a five-year period, for services rendered to the Republican party by business PACs and other forms of corporate financing and endorsements during the 1980 presidential campaign.

From Reagan's perspective, that reduction in personal and corporate taxes was a positive act because it reduced the amount of money available to the government that otherwise might have been spent on unwanted social programs. With ERTA on the books, the federal government lost an estimated $600 billion in tax revenues by 1986. Meanwhile, Congress, in a politically astute move, included in ERTA a system of indexing, not only to offset bracket creep, but to prevent liberal Democrats from using inflation as an argument to challenge those rate changes deemed by Reagan to be such a vital part of his program for economic growth.

Reagan's desire to roll back or cut governmental services was just as intense as his support of a tax cut. In his mind, each was an integral part of the larger process of liberating the private sector and individual initiative from the nefarious grip of big government and its attendant bureaucracies. He had, after all, campaigned in 1980 on the theme of "getting government off our backs." This message was well received across the country, especially with those audiences least in need of governmental support and help for personal and social survival.

David Stockman, always more of a Reaganite than Reagan, took the president's obsession with reducing the role and function of government as a point of departure for policymaking. He quickly proceeded to slash spending on many Great Society programs, believing in the practical necessity of stripping them to their bare bones or cutting off their funding entirely within one budget year. Thus, with Stockman providing the budgetary goals and programmatic direction, Congress, though not going nearly as far as he wanted, cut over $35 billion from the federal budget for fiscal year 1982, and a total of $140 billion through fiscal year 1985, via the Omnibus Budget and Reconciliation Act of 1981. Like the tax cut, OBRA also went to the heart of the Reagan Revolution, positing the legislative need for either axing current programs or reducing their funding on the grounds that such cuts, though unpleasant, were necessary in order to balance the budget.

Predictably, then, those welfare programs that assisted the working or dependent poor got short shrift. Since Reagan had promised earlier to provide a "social safety net" for the needy, some programs were hit harder than others, especially those that provided much-needed help to people already holding a job but whose income placed them slightly above the poverty line. Though funding for the blind, the handicapped, and Medicaid was spared from an all-out attack, the Food Stamp and Aid for Dependent Children programs were cut back or terminated for those whose income levels placed them above the government's poverty line. In addition, there were major spending cuts in programs designed to provide governmental assistance for the poor in the areas of employment, education, public housing, and social welfare. Working mothers who received AFDC checks had their taxes raised to a 60 percent marginal rate when their income levels exceeded the government's definition of poverty. As Douglas Hibbs notes, it was a rate that was higher than that "faced by millionaires under ERTA."

Once OBRA cleared Congress, it was signed into law by President Reagan on August 13, 1981. This legislation marked a major turning point in the recent social history of the United States, going far to reduce or abolish governmental support for the most politically unpopular Great Society programs of the sixties, at a time when the United States already possessed the weakest and most stingily funded welfare state among any of the major industrial democracies of the West. Along with ERTA, it served notice that the United States government, under Ronald Reagan's symbolic leadership, was well disposed to aid and support the most powerful and wealthy elements in the country at the expense of those least able to fend for themselves. Such was the new economic and social gospel according to those supply-siders and the many neoconservative intellectuals located in the White House, the various conservative think tanks, and universities across the country.

Several years after this legislation was enacted, Nathan Glazer, a thoughtful neoconservative, made a reasonable argument that the Reagan administration had not pulled the plug on the welfare state; in fact, many programs dating back to the New Deal still remained intact. Furthermore, the spending cuts directed at social programs had not been all that extreme. Admitting that the poor took the biggest hit, he pointed out that there was no longer a national consensus behind the social engineering approach to welfare policy that had existed in the sixties and early seventies. In his view, that consensus had collapsed because the government's earlier approach to solving the social problems of the urban ghetto had not worked very well: street crime was on the increase, and the welfare system appeared to be in a mess, doing more damage than good.

According to George Gilder, traditional norms of personal responsibility and family accountability, as well as market incentives, had to be at the core of any viable strategy designed to cope with the bleak environment of the poor. As Gilder saw the problem, those who emphasized conservative family values and a proper work ethic had a far better understanding of the limits of social policy than did the welfare-minded liberals of the sixties whose engineering outlook, he argued, had made everything worse.

Charles Murray agreed with Gilder, and he offered in *Losing Ground* a biting attack on Great Society liberalism that became a sourcebook and a key primer on social policy for Reagan conservatives. Murray's book, published in 1984, sought to provide empirical evidence and philosophical grounding for the argument that the welfare programs of the sixties had—as Gilder asserted—indeed impoverished the poor. The crux of his argument was that those programs had made it easier for workers to leave the labor market, thereby ensuring the persistence of poverty and the perpetuation of antisocial behavior. Only by radically reducing such welfare incentives would it be possible, Murray claimed, to reduce crime and family disintegration in urban America. He argued that the market, not welfare, was the appropriate way to cope with the social squalor of the poor in America.

Michael Harrington took strong exception to Murray's model and use of evidence; he argued that by placing the onus for the persistence of poverty on the poverty programs of the sixties, Murray had failed to note that there were other complex factors at work which would better explain why people were unemployed. They included the globalization of the American economy, the acceleration of technological change, and the structural rise in "normal" unemployment. Harrington also pointed out that the welfare state, which Murray had held responsible for causing people to leave the labor market, was already so poorly funded that by 1982 less than half the jobless "received any benefits at all." And he further observed that the benefits that were received from food stamps and AFDC in 1982 "were worth less than one half of AFDC benefits alone in 1969."

Harrington's data revealed incontestably that Reagan had delivered a sharp blow to Lyndon Johnson's War on Poverty programs. Yet as Glazer had pointed out, Reagan was careful, at the same time, to avoid a full-scale challenge to the existing system of social supports. He rejected, for example, a key Senate committee's informal commitment in the spring of 1981 to contain or roll back cost of living allowances (COLAs) for such programs as Social Security, which had solid middle-class backing and strong constituency support in Congress. And despite his feeling that a voluntary approach to Social Security was not such a bad idea, he later backed away from directly challenging the program itself, agreeing in 1983 to reform, not abolition, of the current system. Reagan clearly understood that there were certain political realities that could not be ignored—unlike Stockman, who, as a fully committed conservative ideologue, wanted to abolish virtually every social program within reach of his pen and calculator.

After Stockman left governmental service in the mid-eighties, he expressed his deep disappointment with Reagan, decrying his inability to keep a steady focus on intricate fiscal and budgetary matters. More important was Stockman's argument that because the president was a consensus politician, not an ideologue, he lacked the requisite commitment and passion to undertake the long-term struggle to dismantle the welfare state. As Irving Howe points out, Stockman failed to understand that Reagan was both a practical politician and an ideologue, who recognized that if he clung to his maximum program, he might not even get his minimum. And after his success of 1981, which Stockman helped to engineer, Reagan got more than his minimum; he substantively changed the way issues were framed and debated inside the American political system. As a result of his vision and political appeal, he was destined to emerge as the Roosevelt of the right.

Reagan, much like FDR, presided over a coalition of disparate interest groups, which had converged in 1980 to support his bid for the White House. Of the various groups now situated inside the Reagan tent, the power and needs of the American business community clearly mattered the most to the Reagan White House. It had already given more tax breaks to business than any other administration since the end of World War II; now it was prepared to do even more to restore business confidence and profits, at a time when productivity and growth rates were at a very low ebb. Hence, the Reagan administration broke with the informal working arrangements that had largely characterized government-business-labor relations of the sixties and seventies: it now deliberately sought to undercut, if not destroy, the position and authority of organized labor in order to weaken its bargaining position vis-à-vis business.

A major step in that direction was taken in August 1981 when President Reagan broke the back of the air traffic controllers' union (PATCO) after it had launched an illegal strike against the government. By moving very quickly to decertify this union, which had supported his election bid in 1980, Reagan served notice to the country that a new day in government-labor-management relations had dawned. Organized labor would no longer have privileged entrée into the inner sanctum of government, as had formerly been the case beginning in the 1930s. Nor would its claims be given serious respect or consideration from an administration eager to convert the National Labor Relations Board into an adjunct of business. Labor's failure or inability to contest Reagan's antiunion moves was a fresh indication of the depth of the current crisis of American liberalism, a crisis that preceded the Carter years and was magnified by the events of the Reagan era.

Aided in a major way by the fierce recession of 1981–82, efforts by the Reagan administration to reduce labor costs soon paid off: wage rates began to fall and strikes declined dramatically, both in number and in longevity. As Vogel points out, labor costs dropped by nearly 6 percent in 1983 as compared to the period 1973 to 1981; wage settlements were soon at their lowest since 1968; and strikes in 1982 had dropped to a level that had not been seen since 1945. Clearly, these developments were welcomed by business and the Reagan administration alike, as both hoped that lower operating costs would make American firms more competitive at home and abroad.

Plans to deregulate the American economy were also high on the administration's agenda to help business. For years Reagan himself had been saying that government had "overspent, overestimated, and overregulated." And Murray Weidenbaum, Reagan's first chairman of the White House Council of Economic Advisers, had earlier authored a report for the American Enterprise Institute suggesting that the myriad governmental rules and regulations affecting business were costing $100 billion a year. The time had arrived, he believed, to give business the freedom it needed to invest and plan without always having to look apprehensively over its shoulder in the direction of Washington. Hence, with such a powerful ideological current running inside the administration and Congress, deregulation was now clearly the right cause to champion.

Thus, building on the legacy of Jimmy Carter, who had earlier pursued the deregulation of the airline and trucking industries, the White House sought to free the market from what it considered to be a variety of unnecessary restraints imposed on business by governmental regulatory agencies. It moved, accordingly, to weaken the regulatory reach and authority of a number of key agencies, including the Occupational Safety and Health Administration and the Environmental Protection Agency, by reducing their budgets and staff. In addition, it worked hard to simplify and reduce the number of rules and regulations, numbering in the thousands, with which business had to comply. At the same time, it staffed other key regulatory agencies, including the Federal Trade Commission and the Federal Communications Commission, with people sympathetic to its point of view and goals. Those appointments were clearly made with the intention of promoting the Reagan agenda from the inside out.

Congress, responding to the public mood, sought to hamstring the operations of the Federal Trade Commission; it also passed legislation, with the administration's blessings, that granted the savings and loan industry the freedom to move into the area of commercial banking, a freedom it had never before possessed. So, as Reagan intended, market forces appeared to be liberated from the reach of allegedly officious federal bureaucrats, responsible for impairing business efficiency and raising costs with their all-too-relentless application of rules and regulations on behalf of consumers and workers.

In the late eighties, William Niskanen, a one-time member of Reagan's Council of Economic Advisers, remarked that there had been "little deregulation" in the Reagan years. Himself a committed deregulator, he was clearly expressing his disappointment with the results that had been achieved. Little or not, the Reagan administration produced administrative changes favoring business that worked to weaken health and safety standards for workers, and it managed to push aside all efforts to put new safety equipment into cars by 1983.

But whether David Stockman's "regulatory time bomb," as he labeled the process to limit business autonomy via governmental restrictions, had been defused was another question.

Administration policies, much to the consternation of free-market conservatives, evoked a powerful backlash from environmental groups. Led by the Sierra Club, which had been mobilized by reports of scandal and corruption in the Environmental Protection Agency and efforts by the Department of Interior to open federal lands in the West to large-scale economic development, they managed to hold the administration at bay. By 1983 the momentum had gone out of the deregulation movement, with Congress and the public no longer quite so willing to tolerate the environmental abuses now clearly associated with Reagan administration policies. And as the antiregulatory mood began to pass, congressional efforts to restrain the alleged regulatory excesses of the Federal Trade Commission also subsided. Concurrently, the Reagan administration reached the point where it no longer could slash the budgets and personnel of the regulatory agencies in the same Stockman-like manner as before. Thus, the politics of the regulatory state, tied to the influence and money of the public interest lobby in Congress, prevented the wholesale evisceration of the Johnson-Nixon social regulatory programs, much in the same way that the power and money of business made possible a successful attack on those programs in the late seventies and early eighties.

Meanwhile, Reagan prepared to mount his own attack on inflation, which for most citizens was the economic scourge of the day. Inflation, after all, had virtually destroyed Jimmy Carter's presidency, calling into question the ability of the Democrats to manage the economy in a way that benefited the larger interests of society. Inflation also nurtured the tax revolt of the haves, giving Reagan his opening to argue repeatedly during the 1980 campaign that it was the growing governmental deficit that was responsible for fueling inflation in the first place. Such was the power of the conventional wisdom of the day that Reagan's argument, which Carter had also advanced, was not seriously challenged until Secretary of the Treasury Donald Regan declared in 1983, at the time of the administration's mounting deficit, that there was no necessary or intrinsic connection between the two. In taking this position, Regan now found himself agreeing with Kenneth Arrow, a Nobel laureate in economics, who had said earlier that deficits per se did not create inflation.

Rhetoric aside, a majority of Americans in 1981 thought that inflation was their number one problem; based on the high and persistent inflation rates of 1980–81, they had good reason to believe it. Thus aware of their concerns, President Reagan was eager to wrestle this monster to the ground—and he was prepared to pay the political and economic price to defeat it. Convinced that the country had to take strong medicine after what he called its thirty-year "binge," which he associated with wasteful governmental spending and Great Society programs, Reagan felt confident that a hard-line monetarist approach would go far to lick inflation, allowing him to reach his twin goals of economic stability and noninflationary growth in time for the 1984 election. That is, Reagan, unlike some supply-siders in and out of his administration, was prepared to crush inflation by supporting Federal Reserve Board chairman Paul Volcker's tactics of raising interest rates and tightening the money supply in the belief that the end result would justify the means.

By pushing up interest rates and cutting back on the money supply, Volcker ultimately got what he wanted: inflation declined sharply from 10.4 percent during the 1980–81 period to 6.1 percent in 1982 and 3.2 percent in 1983, but his approach produced a deep recession, representing the most painful economic slide since the thirties. In 1982, the GNP declined a staggering 2.1 percent; business failures that same year numbered 25,000, reaching 31,000 in 1983. Meanwhile, unemployment jumped to 9.5 percent, leaving over 10 million people without work; wages and salaries nosedived; and strikes virtually ceased in a business climate that had produced the greatest number of bank failures since 1940.

Yet the administration—having simultaneously reduced inflation and labor costs—achieved the results that it believed were necessary for restoring a more stable environment for growth and profits. So if the Volckerite "cold bath" had been a deliberate attempt to squeeze inflation out of the system, it came at a great price for American workers whose purchasing power had been declining since 1973. Additionally, as a result of a higher-priced dollar created by Volcker's policy, a balance of trade deficit was pushed from $25.5 billion in 1980 to $123 billion in 1984. Such was the "pain" that Ronald Reagan thought the country had to endure so that Volcker could get the job done.

As the recession began to wreak havoc on business and workers alike, Reagan's standing with the public began to decline, dropping to a 35 percent approval rating by early 1983. Furthermore, poll data revealed that a majority of Americans felt that the tax cut of 1981 was unfair, providing benefits to the rich at the expense of workers and the middle class. Given those developments, the Democrats seemed to be well positioned in 1982 to recover some of the ground they had lost in the disastrous election of 1980. But the political and organizational challenges mounted by the GOP were now daunting in character. And the Democrats had not yet found a way to overcome the deepening racial and ideological divisions inside their own party, which had already gone far to fragment a once powerful majoritarian coalition into different and often opposing interest groups and factions that no longer shared a common national agenda or purpose.

The Republicans recognized more quickly than did the Democrats the critical importance of money and technology in promoting their political success. Well funded and extremely sophisticated about how to disseminate their message to waiting consumers, GOP consultants and party insiders, like Lee Atwater, understood that the medium was the message. Hence, through the adroit use of television and computerized contacts, they offered to carefully selected blocs of voters party views that nicely coincided with, and were reinforced by, material taken from polling firms and focus groups. Possessing such a superior technological edge in the art of political promotion and salesmanship, the GOP knew the rules of a game the Democrats had not yet learned to play.

Too, the GOP benefited from its extraordinary capacity to raise large sums of money to fuel its campaign efforts. Aided by experienced fundraisers with good contacts, the party knew where to go and what to do to get the bucks, concentrating on direct mail solicitations. And its efforts paid off. Going into the 1982 campaign, Republican political fundraising committees had received $214.9 million, as compared to $39 million for the Democrats, giving them virtually a five to one advantage. Also, corporate PACs largely favored Republican congressional candidates, as business at this point still sought to strengthen its own position in Congress by electing them rather than working in tandem with incumbent Democrats.

Meanwhile, the Democrats had one overriding issue to counteract the built-in Republican advantages of money and a superior organization, namely, the state of the economy. Yet they had nothing to offer those now tens of thousands of unemployed workers in the northeastern and midwestern rust belt, who had been displaced by the new global marketplace. Locked in by their fear of inflation and Reagan's burgeoning deficit, Democrats, not knowing what to do, largely avoided discussing alternatives to the economic crisis of the day. Adding to their caution were polls that informed them that though they could still safely attack the rich, it was now politically unwise for Democrats to defend the poor. Alas for the Democrats, the rich voted, though mostly for Republicans, and the poor usually stayed at home.

The Democrats, lacking a program and a leader of national standing, had clearly ceded the national agenda to the White House; nothing revealed the party's futility and impotence more than its endorsement of a balanced budget. For years Democrats had used deficits to fund social programs to which they were committed. But for them to propose new spending programs in the face of Reagan's own rapidly growing deficit would now be a politically dangerous undertaking. Clearly, the Stockman strategy of using the deficit to contain or roll back the welfare state had taken sufficient hold to force the Democrats to modify somewhat their earlier budgetary commitments to sixties welfarism, which was already in a weakened state as a result of the 1980 election. On the other hand, those same Democrats rallied to an all-out defense of Social Security, a universal program that was associated in the minds of most voters with the middle class. Not stigmatized as a means-tested program designed solely for the welfare poor, it was seen as a good welfare program, one that most older Americans, who were serious voters, were prepared to defend with their ballots.

Having lost the power to set the national political agenda, the Democrats also had serious problems with money. Not only did they have far less at their disposal than the GOP but their sources of financial support were more equally divided between organized labor and business. And that split in funding went far to ensure that the party itself, especially in Congress, operated at cross-purposes with respect to policy initiatives and programs. Out of necessity, then, Democrats found it in their political interest not only to forgo a serious challenge to Reaganomics but, at the same time, to seek financial help from precisely those corporate interests who were out to defeat them in the midterm election of 1982.

Yet despite those many drawbacks, the Democrats—profiting from the Reagan recession and their own staunch defense of Social Security—won back twenty-six seats in the House, which effectively frustrated the hopes of Reagan conservatives to realign national politics in their favor. Not surprisingly, the region that provided the Democrats with their greatest support was the Midwest, where structural unemployment had ravaged community after community. At the same time, though, the Republicans staved off a much worse defeat by targeting races across the country that were deemed tossups. They poured money into those closely contested districts via television advertising, thereby preventing the possible loss of another twenty-five or more House seats. Meanwhile, the Democrats used their scarce resources to protect safe and secure incumbents, like Congressman Dan Rostenkowski of Illinois; more marginal candidates for House seats suffered defeat because they received little or no help from the national party organization, which lacked not only the money but the authority and coordinating and centralizing function of the Republican National Committee.

Both sides could take heart from the 1982 returns. Centrist Democrats strengthened their control of the House sufficiently to function as a countervailing force to the bipartisan conservative bloc that had pushed the Reagan legislative package through that chamber during the 1981–82 session. So if House Democrats lacked a viable domestic agenda, they now possessed sufficient voting muscle to prevent Reagan from getting his way again. Hence, the massive budgetary cuts in domestic social programs that took place during Reagan's first two years in office were now a thing of the past. In legislative terms, then, the Reagan Revolution had ground to a halt, at a time when proposals to strengthen environmental laws and new regulatory initiatives were picking up fresh support in Congress.

Despite those Democratic gains in the House, the Republicans managed to win two more Senate seats, adding to their majority in that chamber. Furthermore, Republicans were still in a dominant legislative position in that the Reagan deficits were now so large that they effectively stymied moves by liberals to renew the debate about social policy. In the meantime, Reagan himself was shrewdly calling for a constitutional amendment to balance the budget in order to prevent "big-spending liberals" from again grabbing on to the purse strings of government. Finally, the Republicans could take considerable consolation in knowing that most Democratic gains resulted from a poor economy, and that not all regions had been as hard hit as the industrial and agricultural Midwest. A period of solid economic growth, coupled with a steady decline in inflation, would surely improve Republican chances in 1984, especially since the GOP already had so many social issues, such as affirmative action and abortion, working to its advantage.

Recognizing the importance of the economy to its future prospects, the White House pressured Paul Volcker to remove his foot from the monetary brake in order to allow interest rates to fall and the money supply to grow. In mid-1982, he complied, not only to help the administration but, at the same time, to avoid a catastrophe in Mexico, which was facing the prospect of an imminent financial default resulting from the extremely high interest rates it had to pay on its huge debt owed to many important New York banks.

In early 1983, military spending, a decline in interest rates, and an increase in the money supply fueled an economic upturn. In addition, a timely collapse of the OPEC cartel's high oil prices, along with other factors, helped to lower the inflation rate to under 4 percent. Such was the nature of the recovery that President Reagan, with glad tidings to spread, began to scoff at those who had earlier decried Reaganomics as a producer of bad times. And he soon persuaded the country that something good was happening. After all, most people, following the dismal economic performance of 1981–82, would see any improvement in a positive light. Given the pickup that started in 1983, the White House clearly had fiscal and monetary policy working together to ensure that a fresh Republican political business cycle would happily coincide with the 1984 election. If a large deficit helped to further that business expansion, it could be excused, in Reagan's words, as "a necessary evil" to overcome the effects of the "Carter" recession. As he knew, a majority of voters would not mind the deficit so long as the economic curve was going up, not down.

A dynamic surge of entrepreneurship and eighties-style ostentation soon converged, thanks to the new mood of optimism unleashed by the Reagan boom. As John Kennedy's victory in 1960 had opened space on the left for a host of emerging liberal-radical ideologies and movements, so too did Reagan's rhetoric and politics provide an opportunity and the context for the emergence of new men of power, wealth, and connections, who would thrive in an economic climate that he did much to create. Indeed, the tax cut of 1981, the high interest rates of 1981–82, and the growing federal deficit went far to generate new sources of wealth for those who already had more money than virtually everyone else in America. It is no surprise, then, that since a redistribution of wealth in an upward direction had been a major goal of Reaganomics, the chief beneficiaries were those already at the top of the income pyramid.

The tax cut of 1981 had dropped the top rates from 70 to 50 percent; Volcker's high interest rates helped to squeeze inflation out of the system, but they primarily benefited bondholders and banks; and the growing deficit turned out to be a windfall for the rich because it necessitated a massive selling of Treasury notes, which guaranteed high rates of return to those possessing the funds to purchase them. As a result of these three interconnected developments, anywhere from $120 billion to $160 billion per annum was transferred in the decade of the eighties to the wealthiest 5 percent in America. At the same time, Reaganomics ensured that by the end of the decade one percent of America's families would end up owning or controlling 37 percent of the country's wealth, which was a degree of concentrated economic power and privilege that had not seen since before the New Deal.

Kevin Phillips captured the special political qualities of this new plutocratic era when he wrote: "Millionaire poverty consultants, Southampton seaside benefits for Mexican grape pickers, and Ford Foundation traveling grants for Democratic campaign aides were old news, the elites and perquisites of a bygone era. Now there were Southern California 'kitchen cabinet' cliques, Manhattan and Capitol Hill think tanks promoting tax cuts, Republican fund-raising dinners featuring corporate raiders like Boone Pickens and Ivan Boesky, and Calvin Coolidge birthday parties hosted by parvenu Washington lobbyists and consultants happy to tell attending gossip columnists the price of their new Savile Row suits."

While such Republican political consultants as Roger Stone and Charles Black put Washington under their spell, a variety of business enterprises, such as high tech computer companies, military firms, and deregulated financial institutions, were busily fashioning new forms of wealth in the Sunbelt and elsewhere. Those developments helped to provide a jump-start for the rest of the economy, which was now sufficiently stimulated in 1983–84 to generate a major upturn in jobs and profits.

As all the economic indicators revealed, the Reagan recovery of 1983–84 was exceptionally strong. The jump in the GNP was substantial, and after-tax corporate profits were impressive, amounting to over 7 percent in 1984. Also, the growth in real disposable income for the first three-quarters of that year stood at 5.2 percent, which was the best since 1964. Another important indication that the recession had ended was that nearly five million people found jobs between early 1983 and the late summer of 1984.

The fact that so many people were now back at work was good news. Yet, a large number were employed in the service sector of the economy, where people were generally hired at the minimum wage level in a nonunionized setting. Meanwhile, as a result of global competition and the increasing computerizing or robotizing of work itself, millions of well-paying semiskilled or unskilled manufacturing jobs that Americans had once taken for granted disappeared in the eighties. Despite the return of substantial growth and high corporate profits, a dual economy was rapidly emerging in the Reagan era, which in turn provided high-paying jobs for a well-educated, technically competent elite. But there were only dead-end entry level jobs at McDonald's and Burger King for millions of other uneducated, politically marginalized individuals, which meant that their ticket into the middle class had been permanently lost.

In the meantime, a substantial number of lower middle-class families survived Reaganomics only because both the husband and wife had jobs. Although conservative critics were quick to decry the presence of so many mothers in the work force, charging them with disregarding their family responsibilities, those same mothers brought home dollars that, in many cases, prevented their families from suffering a sharp decline in living standards. Economist Mark Levinson notes that the average American family, in the period from 1979 to 1987, had an income decline of between 4 percent and 6.5 percent unless another adult from that same family also entered the labor market. By 1986, the personal indebtedness of the average American family, excluding mortgages, had risen to more than $11,500, forcing it, by one estimation, to spend one-fifth of its monthly income on debt payments alone.

Although the deficit-driven and debt-ridden economy had powered the Reagan recovery, serious problems remained, which the White House was now in a good political position to ignore or easily to brush aside. After all, for example, although unemployment in 1984 stood at 7.5 percent, just as it had in 1980, many people were once more back at work following the terrible downturn of the 1981–82 period. If growth during the 1981–84 period averaged only

2.7 percent, which was a half point below the figure for the seventies, the extraordinary spurt of 1983–84 is what mattered to the White House over the short political term preceding the election. And if the tax cut of 1981 especially benefited those in the top income brackets, couples in the middle income brackets, who were often in a strategic voting position to decide national elections, also saw a slight improvement in their take-home pay since the Reagan cut of 1981. Data released at the end of the decade by the Congressional Budget Office showed that even though those families in the top one percent of income earners gained an estimated $186,022 (as measured in 1990 dollars), a majority of working families in America, in Thomas Edsall's words, "were not net losers." That fact alone complicated the problems of the national Democratic party, which was now searching desperately for a viable political and economic alternative to Reaganomics.

Meanwhile, Reagan stood to benefit politically for having helped to exorcise an economic ogre that had been a major concern of many people for a long time: inflation. The vicious inflationary cycle of the seventies had been broken as a result of the brutal recession of 1981–82, thereby initiating a period of mild inflation of no more than 4 percent to 5 percent a year. Most voters tended to worry more about inflation than unemployment, and they remembered only too well the years of double-digit inflation that in their minds were rightfully associated with the Carter presidency. Thus, Reagan's own solid economic performance since 1983, including his successful battle against high inflation, went far to improve his chances of holding on to the White House in 1984.

Although that economic rebound gave Reagan another opportunity to kick Jimmy Carter around, his show of resolve and determination in foreign affairs also did much to reassure the electorate. His approach provided exactly the mix that most voters wanted. He denounced the Soviet Union as an "evil empire" whose strategic challenge to American security necessitated a massive increase in American military power, but he was careful to avoid a major military engagement like Vietnam that might arouse the voters' ire. Thus operating in a politically astute manner, Reagan gave his television audience a superlative military victory in Grenada, which cost very little in a material sense, and he ordered the troops out of Beirut after 241 Marines had been killed by a suicidal bomb attack on their barracks.

In the meantime, Reagan enthusiastically embraced two foreign policy objectives: support for the Contra opponents of the Sandinista regime in Nicaragua, and a staunch commitment to the Strategic Defense Initiative (SDI), or "star wars." He viewed the Contras as "the moral equal of our Founding Fathers," and he saw SDI functioning as a massive security shield that would go far to protect the American people from total nuclear devastation in the event of war with the Soviet Union. Although a majority of Americans opposed military aid for the Contras, and many luminaries in the scientific establishment thought that Reagan's star wars concept was at best fanciful, conservatives promptly endorsed both proposals, and, in the name of a militant anticommunism and American globalism, mobilized vast political and financial resources on their behalf.

Reagan's domestic policies inspired similar loyalty and support from people who could be classified as Reagan Democrats. For instance, many working-class and lower-middle-class whites, whose political loyalties went back to Franklin Roosevelt, closely identified with his attack on big government and his demand for lower taxes, for these perspectives captured well their own changing attitudes toward the welfare state and race. Like many others, they were tired of seeing their tax dollars spent on poor blacks, who did not seem to benefit from the various welfare programs sponsored by the government: black street crime was still very much on the increase, while the inner cities continued to rot away.

Reagan was also helped by the fact that many of those same whites resented the Democratic liberal establishment. They believed that its policies were responsible for having forced housing and school integration on them in such a way that control of their own neighborhoods and schools was now being threatened by a black invasion. And they also condemned that same liberal establishment for having initiated those affirmative action programs that, in their view, had undermined the integrity of meritocratic hiring procedures in both the public and the private sectors of the American economy. Because of their various social and economic concerns, as well as fears about their own personal safety, millions of white Americans responded positively to Reagan's antigovernmental themes, which were rooted in an ill-disguised attack on the constituency that was so dependent on the system of welfarism in the first place.

Jerry Falwell's Moral Majority and members of the Southern Baptist Convention had their own particular reasons for embracing Reagan. Throughout his first term, the president had publicly opposed abortion and demanded that prayer be put back in the public schools. Even if he was unable to persuade Congress to pass the specific legislation that these conservatives had sought, everyone in the country knew that Ronald Reagan stood by their side on those issues that mattered the most to them. In actuality, however, the political agenda of the New Religious Right was never a priority with this administration. It had other, far more pressing matters to address, including the economy, taxes, and the military buildup. Yet during the course of his first term, Reagan played a good game of symbolic politics with Falwell and his friends by suggesting to them that he was trying to do business on their behalf. His was a useful ploy that kept an important new constituency in line and fully supportive of his reelection bid.

The need to restore confidence in the American business system was at the top of Reagan's agenda, virtually from the first day he took office. And the Business Roundtable, the *Wall Street Journal*, and the American Enterprise Institute were delighted with his performance. Thanks to him, business had benefited from a tax cut, a reduced inflation rate, and a more distinctly antiunion environment than anyone could remember since before the New Deal. Profits soared, and the 1984 election looked like, in the words of one Wall Street insider, "an investment banker's dream world."

The dominant cultural fact emerging from Reagan's first term was that the unabashed quest for money and the sanctioning of individual greed had become more respectable than any time since the boom days of the twenties. Much to the applause of many, Ivan Boesky said that "greed is healthy." Boesky, a leading inside trader who would later be imprisoned for his various Wall Street illegalities and misdeeds, had a perspective that had been sanctioned by Reagan's politics and moral sensibility, which was far removed from the outlook of the sixties and early seventies. At that time, Lyndon Johnson had achieved his great legislative triumphs on behalf of civil rights legislation and various poverty programs; even Richard Nixon continued to fund the welfare state at a relatively high level. Now the social values of a different age clearly held sway, predicated on the working principle that people should, above all, enrich themselves. While the money managers flocked to Wall Street and entrepreneurs to Main Street, the Republicans were busily at work in their political garden, cultivating those wedge issues, tied to race and culture, that they had so successfully used and exploited in 1980.

As the 1984 election approached, the Reagan coalition of 1980 was still intact and growing in strength. As in 1980, it was unified, above all, by its implacable opposition to global communism. Differences on the domestic side, say, between supply-siders and monetarists, or between libertarian conservatives and the New Religious Right, were subordinated to a foreign policy agenda on which all elements were agreed. But notwithstanding their domestic differences, the various factions inside the conservative movement enthusiastically supported Ronald Reagan's bid for reelection. They understood that unless he retained power their chances of achieving certain objectives, including a massive revamping of liberal welfare policies, the repudiation of affirmative action programs, and the appointment of politically and ideologically correct judges to the federal judiciary, would be blocked by the return of Democrats to the White House.

Democrats, having made a good recovery in the midterm election of 1982, thought that they now had sufficient political momentum to face the challenge of the 1984 election. But once the campaign for the party's nomination began, they soon found themselves, like Caesar's Gaul, divided into three parts; unlike Gaul, however, they had to face Ronald Reagan, not Julius Caesar. On the party's left was a faction led by the Reverend Jesse Jackson, an associate of the late Martin Luther King, Jr. Representing an emerging neoliberal bloc was Senator Gary Hart of Colorado. And former vice-president Walter Mondale, a protégé of the late Hubert Humphrey, represented organized labor and the party's traditional centrist establishment. Though each candidate had specific plans and programs for coping with the political and ideological crisis that had enveloped the Democratic party ever since the collapse of the New Deal order, it was highly questionable as to whether their respective alternatives to a Reagan-dominated policy agenda would appeal to voting Americans in a period of solid economic recovery at home and a favorable reassertion of American power abroad.

Jesse Jackson, encouraged by Harold Washington's successful bid to become the first black mayor of Chicago, entered the race to rally his supporters and the party faithful around a program of social reform that sought to address the serious economic problems faced by poor blacks and whites, who had not benefited from the Reagan recovery. Thus speaking for his "Rainbow Coalition"—a patchwork political creation of Hispanics, feminists, anti-interventionists, left-liberals, black militants, and labor radicals—Jackson strongly endorsed a program of massive social reconstruction via the restoration of the Reagan cuts in welfare programs and a huge public works program designed to rebuild the rotting cities of America.

Jackson's efforts to fashion a viable left policy inside the Democratic party were compromised, indeed seriously hurt, by the fact that he had had a close working relationship with Louis Farrakhan, a black minister with a virulent anti-Semitic bias. In the course of his campaign for the nomination, Jackson had referred to New York City as "Hymietown," which he later denied having said. In addition, his cozy relationship with such third world dictators as Fidel Castro did little to endear him to most rank-and-file Democrats. Yet Jackson, to his credit, dared to challenge the continuing conservative drift inside the Democratic party by raising aloft, once more, the torn and tattered flag of left-liberalism.

Another flag, with a totally different ideological coloration, was hoisted by Senator Gary Hart, a leading spokesman for those forces inside the Democratic party who largely shared Reagan's belief in the efficacy of the market and the virtues of the private sector. Building on the political legacy of former California governor Jerry Brown, Hart largely brushed aside the problems of the working poor and the decline of the midwestern industrial heartland, proposing that the Democratic party commit itself to supporting the new high tech industries that had come of age in such places as California's Silicon Valley. As a leading neoliberal, Hart thus washed his hands of the old liberal-labor coalition, which had been a dominant element in the national Democratic party since the Roosevelt years. Instead, he banked his hopes for the nomination on a younger group of voters, who embodied the political outlook of the "Big Chill" generation: that is, a generation that was committed to social libertarianism, economic opportunity, and upward mobility at home and the politics of noninterventionism abroad. Despite his spirited campaign on behalf of what seemed to be a new political agenda for the Democratic party, Hart's effort to win the nomination fell short, as he lost key primary battles, including a decisive showdown in Illinois, to Walter Mondale, the party's eventual nominee.

Mondale was the candidate of choice for the tattered remains of the liberal-labor coalition. The AFL-CIO Executive Council had endorsed him very early in the primary season, because, among other reasons, it was pleased with his commitment (later suspended) to an industrial policy of sorts that envisioned via state sponsorship the rebuilding of the manufacturing sector of the American economy on terms favorable to organized labor. At the same time, though, Mondale supported some of Reagan's cutbacks in social spending, generally went along with his arms buildup, approved of his invasion of Grenada, and agreed that it was necessary to contain any radical threat to American interests emanating from Managua.

In a concerted effort to shore up his position with important Democrats, Mondale sought to build bridges to the party's various interest groups, including those organized by women, blacks, and labor. With their help, he locked up the nomination via the primary route well before the party's convention met in San Francisco. During that July convention, he made American political history by selecting Congresswoman Geraldine Ferraro, an Italian Catholic from New York, to be his running mate. Mondale clearly hoped to exploit the so-called gender gap to his advantage. Little did he know at the time, however, that this bold move would cause him acute embarrassment: he was later hurt by the revelation that the financial statement that Ferraro had submitted to the House, pertaining to her campaign for Congress in 1978, was inaccurate and misleading and that she had spent a vast amount of her husband's money to help her win that election, which was a direct violation of existing federal campaign rules and regulations governing the size of family contributions to a political campaign.

Mondale's biggest mistake was not his selection of Geraldine Ferraro but the declaration contained in his acceptance speech that, if elected, he would raise taxes in order to cope with the massive Reagan deficit. As he put it: "I mean business. By the end of my first term, I will cut the deficit by two-thirds. Let's tell the truth. Mr. Reagan will raise taxes, and so will I. He won't tell you. I just did." It was a commitment that played right into Reagan's hands. For one thing, most Americans did not worry about the deficit; for another, they feared that a tax hike would be used to obtain revenues for costly new federal programs for the black poor, programs that they largely opposed. In addition, by attacking the deficit in the manner that he did, Mondale gave away the major fiscal tool that Democrats had employed for years to justify their existence as Democrats, not Republicans. Thanks first to Carter and now to Mondale, deficit reduction, not growth and prosperity, appeared to be what the Democrats had in mind as an economic alternative to Republicans of the Reagan persuasion.

Clearly, the national Democratic party was in deep crisis. And though Jackson, Hart, and Mondale had each offered specific programs and approaches to confront it, their pointed disagreements over substantive matters went far to highlight two major difficulties Democrats now faced in the age of Reagan. First, the party lacked any consensus or program to deal with the globalization of the American economy. Second, it had no way to cope politically with the problems associated with either the growing black underclass or the increasingly bitter racial and gender conflicts over affirmative action programs without destroying the party's once-solid white working-class base. By 1984 the national Democratic party, which had once served as the safe harbor for welfare state liberalism, was adrift on a sea of ideological confusion while facing the likely prospect of another political defeat in November.

Meanwhile, confident conservatives were speaking with the only voice (Reagan's) a vast majority of voting Americans wanted to hear. After being renominated at the Republican party's convention in Dallas, which was totally dominated by conservatives, Reagan and his running mate, George Bush, emphasized the point that it was indeed "Morning Again in America." Such was their campaign theme, and it was merchandised superbly via the media, especially by Reagan. Like no other politician since Franklin Roosevelt, he made very good use of language and sentiment to tap into the wellspring of traditional American beliefs and values, which were associated with an old-fashioned American patriotism, on one hand, and a commitment to free markets and individual opportunity, on the other.

In addition to having made Americans feel good about themselves, Reagan was also helped by a number of other factors that worked in his favor. Most important was the fact that the economic recovery went far to convince a majority of voters that the country's economy was better entrusted to the Republicans than the Democrats. At the same time, Reagan's "leadership" qualities appealed to large numbers of people, who believed that he had brought the country together again by restoring confidence in its political institutions while ensuring that America once more stood "tall" abroad.

Republican senator Bob Dole, a shrewd student of American politics, observed that the GOP faced a serious identity problem without

Reagan. Although Reagan was the charismatic force that Republicans needed to boost their presidential and party prospects, big money and a solid party organization also played a major role in promoting both him and those conservative ideas and causes that he had embraced. As in 1980 and 1982, then, substantial campaign contributions from over two million grass-roots donors filled the coffers of the GOP, allowing it to reach those audiences that had been so carefully targeted and mobilized on behalf of the entire Republican ticket.

According to Lee Atwater, a leading tactician of the Republican party, no region was more important to the GOP than the South. For him the winning of the South was a key to any successful Republican drive to capture the White House. Thus, it was a good omen for the party when ministers associated with the Southern Baptist Convention threw their support to Reagan because of his stand on such issues as abortion and prayer in the public schools. Encouraging, too, for the Republicans was the fact that across the region Reagan benefited from the intense white opposition to affirmative action programs and welfarism. And a fast-growing Republican middle class, which was associated with an increasing suburbanization of southern politics and life, supported his stand on taxes and deregulation. Just as Atwater had hoped, Reagan's appeal below the Mason-Dixon line brought together the two streams of southern conservatism: one was rooted in the working-class, semi-marginalized world of the small town or rural Protestant South; the other was found in the boardrooms and country clubs of the new business-minded South.

Republicans aided their own cause by launching a massive registration drive to counter an ostensibly major push by the Democrats. In fact, over two million new voters of an evangelical or fundamentalist persuasion were added to voter rolls with the help of Jerry Falwell. Ironically, though, the Democratic registration drive stalled, especially among a potential bloc of new black voters, because money for such an effort never materialized, despite Mondale's earlier assurances that such a project would be funded by the party. Evidently party moguls helped to shelve it, fearing that such a mobilization might succeed to the point that their own hold on the party's machinery could be contested by new forces they could not easily control.

Like Richard Nixon's victory in 1972, Ronald Reagan's in 1984 was never in doubt. A high point of the conservative era, the election confirmed that the American people, in the context of an economic upturn, liked their "Gipper," who won 59 percent of the vote and carried every state in the union except Walter Mondale's Minnesota. Despite his landslide, Reagan did not bring a Republican Congress in with him. Even though the GOP managed to pick up a net of 16 seats in the House, the Democrats remained in control of that chamber. Yet the Republicans surely noticed that affluent Americans, who were the prime beneficiaries of the 1981 tax cut, voted in big numbers for the Reagan-Bush ticket, suggesting that their support was very important in preserving Republican presidential hegemony. Republicans also did very well in the 18 to 30 age bracket, indicating that many younger or new voters had picked up the party's message that Republicans, not Democrats, could best protect them from a renewal of inflation and a return to an era of Jimmy Carter-style stagflation. Finally, the election confirmed that the presidential South was now in hands of the Republicans. Such a realignment of political forces had occurred with the help of millions of evangelical and fundamentalist voters, who helped to establish the GOP as the dominant political player in that part of the country.

The Democratic voting base continued to shrink across the country for reasons having to do with apathy, mixed messages, or co-optation by Reagan Republicans. Although blacks and a solid majority of Jews remained loyal to the memory of the older liberalism for which the Democratic party once stood, they did not have the numbers to compensate for a major demographic shift among other Democrats and independents to Reagan. That shift was accelerated by the rapid decline of the organized labor movement, which by 1984 spoke for only 16 percent of all those many millions at work in America. Once a respected and significant force inside the political system, organized labor had been profoundly weakened by the antilabor stance of the Reagan administration, the various forced givebacks, a globalized economy, and the recession of 1982. Thus, the leadership of the AFL-CIO, though it helped to nominate Mondale, was no longer able to muster a big labor vote for Democrats in November as it had, say, in 1968 or 1976. Consequently, some 40 percent of those who were union members and their families voted for Reagan in 1984; they liked his stand on foreign policy and domestic issues and found him to be a leader worthy of their respect.

Labor, after having lost political clout in the arena of presidential politics, also found it difficult to compete effectively with business PACs for the support of congressional Democrats. As money, along with votes, became an essential tool for political survival, Democrats, lacking the donor base of the GOP, needed funding from sources other than labor. House Democrats, led by Congressman Tony Coelho, chairman of the Democratic Congressional Campaign Committee, made it known that they had something to offer corporate America, namely the power of incumbency. If corporate America wanted to protect its interests, Coelho advised it to seek Democratic cooperation via business PACs. Democrats, like Republicans, were quite willing to discuss "capital formation and other business issues" in an open and receptive manner.

Corporate America responded positively to Coelho's urgings that it go along in order to get along. Unlike 1980 and 1982, business supported many more Democratic incumbents in the House, accepting as a given their seemingly secure position of power and their expressed willingness to look favorably at business needs and concerns. As that relationship took hold, organized labor's own bargaining position with key House Democrats changed for the worse. Benefiting politically from their contacts with business lobbyists, those Democrats increasingly turned a deaf ear toward labor lobbyists.

Most Americans now viewed the moribund American labor movement as just another contemptible "special interest," whose condition did not concern them. That widespread attitude and belief was only one more indication of how far Ronald Reagan had succeeded in his first term in changing the national political agenda from one that included a commitment of sorts to the larger concerns of society to one dominated almost solely by the ethic of possessive individualism and the politics of laissez faire. His ideological triumph was such that a majority of voters now thought of Great Society liberalism as simply the chief sponsor of wasteful and useless programs for the black poor, which in turn helped to create a big governmental bureaucracy and a huge federal deficit.

At the same time, Reagan provided benefits for the most important and powerful elements inside his conservative coalition, including Sunbelt entrepreneurs, Wall Street investors, and various interests connected to the Department of Defense. In addition, he appointed conservatives to the federal judiciary in large numbers and staffed the administrative agencies of the federal government with people of a similar ideological persuasion. He also lowered spending on welfare programs and reduced the grants the federal government had given to the cities and states via a decentralized federalism.

Meanwhile, in an era when greed and conspicuous consumption converged to give old money a bad name, a Wall Street boom commenced, and leveraged buyouts became commonplace. Much of this would not have occurred in the manner it did without his election. Not since Franklin Roosevelt had any one president altered the political landscape so radically and in such a short period as had Ronald Reagan. Indeed, his impact on the country had been enormous.

Conservatism in Decline, 1985–1992

Ronald Reagan won a landslide victory in 1984 because millions of voters believed, along with him, that it was "morning again in America." That widespread belief, nurtured by a major economic upturn, helped Republicans to retain the White House and to consolidate their presidential base in the South. Nevertheless, many of those same millions, who reelected Reagan and kept the Republicans in control of the Senate, continued to vote for Democratic incumbents in the House of Representatives. They believed that the Democrats were better able to deliver specific political and economic services that often mattered more to constituents on the local level, while cultural values, foreign policy, and defense issues appeared more important on the level of presidential politics. In an era when the GOP controlled the White House and the Senate (down to 1986), most Democratic House incumbents, with the help of PAC money, were reelected, suggesting that split-level government had become the norm of American political life.

More specifically, that situation prevailed because the Republican party lacked sufficient voter support to produce the political realignment it had sought. Despite Reagan's popularity, and the willingness of many voters to go along with the party's economic and social agenda, the Reagan recession of 1981–82 had given the Democrats in the House a new lease on life, preventing a complete Republican domination of the national government.

Still, the GOP had captured the White House in 1980 and 1984 and had controlled the Senate since 1980, indicating that it had come a long way since the Watergate era. That remarkable comeback had taken place in the context of a changed party. It was no longer the party of northern WASPs; the addition of large numbers of Southern Baptists and upscale northern Catholics, as well as Reagan Democrats, had gone far to transform its political and social composition. As a result of these changes, the presidential wing of the GOP had established deeper roots inside American society than at any time in recent memory.

But the Republican party also included elements whose social agendas conflicted with one another's. Republican libertarians supported Reagan's free-market individualism and applauded his antistatist rhetoric; yet they were decidedly unhappy with the outlook and values of the New Religious Right, which had become an important new player in the politics of the party. It was the religious right that wanted the state to play an active role in legislating morality in the bedroom and schoolroom, though not necessarily in the boardroom. The strong differences in cultural values and outlook that separated libertarian conservatives from Jerry Falwell's supporters was such that the Reagan coalition was rife with tension and not always as stable as it appeared.

In class terms, the Republican party remained essentially the party of upper-middle-class and upper-class Americans, who had been the primary beneficiaries of Reaganomics. They were winners in the redistribution game the Reagan White House had played at the expense of the poor and the lower middle class. As long as the GOP could deliver the semblance, if not the substance, of prosperity to working Americans, a majority of voters were convinced that a Republican president could be better trusted to make the right economic decisions. That same majority, having lived through the foreign policy frustrations and failures of the Carter years, also felt that a Republican president like Reagan could better protect American security interests in a global context.

Meanwhile, the presidential wing of the Democratic party was identified in the minds of many voters across the country as the party of cultural elites and the black poor, whose politics and ideology did not represent mainstream white America. The problems facing the national Democrats also went much deeper: they could not fashion a coherent economic program or deliver a political message that would appeal, concurrently, to blue-collar workers and the black poor, to environmentalists and organized labor, to feminists and cultural conservatives. Unable to transcend those intense political differences and value-laden polarities, the national Democratic party was caught in a web of bitter interest-group conflicts and rivalries from which the only likely escape was a recession akin to that of 1981–82, or something worse.

Money, too, remained a serious problem for the Democrats. The source of their funding was such that they were equally beholden to both organized labor and business, making it all the more difficult for the party to offer a clear message as to where it stood on a variety of political and economic issues. In addition, the Democrats were far too dependent on money coming from an upper-middle-class elite, located in Hollywood and New York, that had little or no interest in promoting such populist causes as increased taxes on the wealthy and a challenge to the power of corporate America.

Because the Reagan White House retained the power to set the national agenda for another four years, it concentrated on issues that had worked for it during the first term, including the economy, taxes, and foreign policy. The dominant political reality facing the administration and Congress after 1984 was the fact that the tax cut of 1981 and the continuing military buildup had created a huge and virtually uncontrollable federal deficit, which by 1985 had grown to $200 billion per year. Although the budget deficit had been a primary factor in pulling the economy out of the 1981–82 slump, it also served the Reagan administration well in that it prevented congressional Democrats from offering new social programs that might have had some appeal for lower-middle-class white voters as well as poor blacks. Meanwhile, as a result of those mounting deficits, the annual interest on the federal debt grew to staggering new heights, climbing from $96 billion in 1981 to $216 billion in 1988. And the major beneficiaries of that development were already very wealthy Americans, or rich foreigners, who were the principal owners of Treasury bonds to whom the federal government was obligated to pay interest for the use of their money.

Congress, worried about the size of the escalating deficit, passed the Gramm-Rudman-Hollings Bill (GRH) in 1985, which was designed to impose a sense of discipline on the budgetary process. It mandated that the federal budget be balanced by 1991, which meant that a massive cutback in federal spending, obviously affecting military appropriations as well as most domestic programs, would be required. Reagan liked GRH because he thought it provided a surefire way to reduce unwanted domestic spending, thereby locking in those

Democrats who were still hoping to finance social programs with fresh appropriations.

Many Democrats, including Senator Edward Kennedy, a staunch Great Society liberal, went along with GRH, hoping to use this process to force the administration to cut military spending, raise taxes, or both. Later, in 1987, after the Supreme Court had ruled that a key provision of the law was unconstitutional, Congress, with strong Democratic backing, passed a modified version of GRH. The new law ensured that the shell game of budgetary politics and deficit reduction, as practiced by Democrats and Republicans alike, would continue unabated into and beyond the 1988 campaign. Yet the newer version of GRH, requiring a mandatory balanced budget by 1993, did constitute something of an improvement over the original measure, since it bought time for the development of other policy initiatives in case they were needed to cope with any future fiscal contingency.

Along with GRH, the administration was eager to proceed with tax reform, which became the key domestic legislative proposal of Reagan's second term. Although the White House was aware that many Americans viewed the 1981 tax act as one-sided, palpably favoring the rich and the corporations, it also knew that such Democrats as Senator Bill Bradley and Congressman Richard Gephardt were preparing their own bill calling for tax reform. Reagan moved quickly to seize the initiative on behalf of his so-called populist agenda, informing Congress on January 25, 1984, that he would offer a plan to simplify the tax code. After the November election, he submitted proposals to Congress, which later formed the basis for the bipartisan negotiations that culminated in the Tax Reform Act of 1986.

The 1986 legislation was driven, in part, by Reagan's desire to reduce the top personal rate well below the 50 percent margin, which had been set by the 1981 legislation. Also, both the White House and Congress agreed to revoke the investment tax credit, which now meant that some firms would have to pay higher taxes than they did under the 1981 law, while others would have their taxes lowered. Significantly, even though this legislation ensured that the amount of revenue collected by Washington from business would remain roughly the same, or even drop, as a result of the new rates, the fight over the tax bill of 1986 split the business community, which had not been the case in 1981 when virtually all sectors of business stood united behind the Reagan tax proposals of that year.

Despite that disagreement, the 1986 bill passed because it appealed to both liberals and conservatives. Supply-siders were pleased that the top marginal rate on personal incomes had been further reduced, from 50 percent to 28 percent (which nearly matched the Coolidge administration's 25 percent, some sixty years earlier), and they supported the reduction in the top corporate rate from 48 percent to 42 percent. Also to their liking was the fact that the various changes incorporated into the 1986 act remained "revenue neutral"; that is, the legislation shifted the burden of taxation but did not increase the current level of taxation.

Congressional Democrats of liberal persuasion went along with this bill because it removed four million of the poorest taxpayers from the rolls, because it managed to increase the taxes of some firms in the business community, and because it denied those who sought a tax break for capital gains the "special treatment" that earlier legislation had given them. Still, that same act was hardly consistent with the moderate progressivity that had characterized tax legislation for the forty years prior to 1981. As Harvard economist Richard Musgrave remarked, the passage of the 1986 act constituted an abandonment of progressivity. In his view, it was "a historic retreat   a drastic change in what Congress views to be the proper distribution of the tax burden."

Democrats, on the run and lacking a viable alternative to Reaganomics, had once again surrendered to the politics and ideology of supply-side economics. But what could they do? Trapped by the huge deficits that the Reagan White House used to spend its way out of the recession of 1981–82, and hurt by Walter Mondale's call for tax hikes in 1984, Democrats were still viewed by a substantial number of voters as "tax and spend" Democrats who had administered a welfare state that had wasted tax dollars on failed programs for ghetto blacks. Yet those were precisely the programs that Democrats needed to sponsor in order to rally their most loyal constituents on election day. Such was their political dilemma at a time when the wedge politics and supply-side nostrums of the Reagan administration had succeeded in giving liberalism not only a bad name but a discredited history.

The failure of the Democrats to restore their one-time hegemony was also due to their failure to note in time that rising taxes, including regressive Social Security taxes, had taken a big bite out of the incomes of lower-middle-class swing voters, who were the object of a concerted Republican campaign to win them over via the politics of cultural and racial resentment. The increase in Social Security taxes, resulting from legislation passed in 1983, was such that the Congressional Budget Office estimated that two-thirds of all American families, counting their employers' share, were giving more by 1991 to the Social Security Administration than to the Internal Revenue Service. But it was the combination of both payroll taxes that tore at individuals making no more than $53,400 a year, which was the cutoff point for an annual Social Security and Medicare contribution of 7.65 percent per salary.

Meanwhile, the administration took pleasure in the fact that the economic news in 1986 remained good and was getting better. The White House could rightfully point out that over eleven million new jobs had been created since 1983, that economic growth was solid and steady, and that inflation was very much under control. In short, President Reagan had clearly delivered the prosperity he had promised the country in 1980 and 1984, suggesting that the people's confidence in his economic management and leadership had not been misplaced.

Although the White House painted a reassuring picture of the American economy, there were serious problems lying just below the surface to indicate that this recovery was not just another conventional upturn in the post–World War II business cycle. It was substantially financed by vast amounts of money coming from abroad, attracted by the high interest rates that Paul Volcker had imposed on the system in order to do battle with inflation. Soon, so much money flowed into the country from the outside to help fund the deficit (totaling an inflow of $90 billion in 1984 alone) that the United States emerged during the Reagan years as the world's largest debtor nation. By 1990, the accumulated overseas debt had grown to such an extent that the annual interest payment on funds borrowed from external sources now exceeded $60 billion.

As the result of those high interest rates, the American dollar also jumped in value on world money markets, making it far more difficult for American exporters to compete internationally—especially against Japan, which had emerged in the seventies and eighties as a powerful rival inside the global economy. The Japanese challenge to America's one-time economic superiority was now so serious that in 1985 Secretary of the Treasury James Baker negotiated a multilateral currency agreement among the major industrial nations of the

West, promoting an upward reevaluation of the Japanese yen and the German mark and the relative lowering of the high-priced American dollar on world markets.

Although that agreement went far to cheapen the American dollar, it did not solve the long-term problem of competitiveness plaguing American industry both at home and overseas. In broad terms, American manufacturing had continued to lose ground since the seventies. For example, America's share of world imports in 1986 had risen to 17.5 percent as compared to 12.9 percent in 1970. At the same time, its share of world exports had fallen from 13.8 percent in 1970 to only 10.3 percent in 1986. In each case, Japan, pursuing an industrial policy that the Reagan administration had so grandly eschewed, gained at America's expense. A leading Japanese economic publication later estimated that by 1987 the country had already surpassed the United States in total national assets, owning $43.7 trillion to America's $36.2 trillion (in U.S. dollars).

At a time when excess capacity already dominated the American manufacturing sector, the decline in global competitiveness played havoc with the hopes of many Americans who no longer could find blue collar jobs to provide a decent standard of living for themselves and their families. Such jobs had started to disappear in the seventies, and by the mid-eighties they were becoming harder and harder to find, even as service sector employment began to expand so dramatically. This meant that the heightened productivity gains of the eighties, which occurred in the manufacturing sector of the economy, were achieved with a work force much diminished in numbers and earning power. Real hourly wages for those manufacturing workers, which had reached almost $9.50 an hour in 1978, had fallen to almost $8.00 an hour by 1990. Despite the economic improvement of the mid-eighties, the stagnation in real incomes, which had commenced for large numbers of employed Americans ever since 1973, had not changed. Median household income—adjusted for inflation —was $29,943 in 1990 dollars, which was $1,000 less than it had been in 1973. Only the top 20 percent of the population, making more than $80,000, managed to avoid a similar long-term decline or stagnation in real income.

Herbert Stein, chief economic adviser to former presidents Richard Nixon and Gerald Ford, observed that many Americans were experiencing a "revolution of declining expectations" during the Reagan era. He pointed out, as paraphrased by Leonard Silk of the *New*

York Times, that "the present inflation rate is twice as high as the average of the years 1947 to 1967, that between 1947 and 1973 there were only two years in which the unemployment rate was as high as in 1987 (6.1 percent) and that between 1980 and 1987 the rate of growth of productivity was half as great as between 1947 and 1973." This was a telling comment coming from a card-carrying Republican economist, but it mattered little to people in the Reagan White House. For them, a better basis of economic comparison was not with the entire post–World War II period but, rather, with the Carter years; on that score, Reagan continued to look good to those Americans who mattered the most to him—a majority of the voters. They associated him with having ended a period of high inflation and with the return of stable economic growth, and they supported his administration's opposition to welfare programs that had been designed to help the black poor, not themselves.

Many of those same voters who had endorsed Reagan's social agenda failed or refused to see that his administration had tolerated or even sanctioned economic behavior that was doing serious damage to the financial and economic infrastructure of the country. Although the Reagan administration did not initiate efforts to deregulate the American economy, it fully supported, along with Congress, a process that led to the further weakening of regulatory oversight in such sectors as the savings and loan (S & L) industry, which had as its major role and function the underwriting of mortgages in the area of residential housing. And it closed its eyes to those antics on Wall Street and elsewhere that inspired the merger movement and paper entrepreneurship of the day, which together seriously hurt efforts to promote the fuller use of capital resources along more productive and less speculative lines.

The savings and loan crisis, which some critics thought could end up costing taxpayers as much as $500 billion over a thirty-year period, emerged from the same political environment that helped to elect Ronald Reagan as president. During the Carter era, members of that industry found themselves in financial trouble at a time of double-digit interest rates. As economist Lawrence Ritter wrote, "Most of their income was derived from long-term fixed-rate mortgages acquired when interest rates were much lower, whereas they had to pay out high interest rates to prevent depositors from withdrawing funds in search of better yield elsewhere." Understandably, industry representatives turned for help to Congress, which, in 1982, via the

Garn–St. Germain Act, obligingly gave them the right to make commercial loans and use their assets in a far less restricted and unregulated manner than before. When President Reagan signed this legislation into law, he called it "the most important legislation for financial institutions in the last fifty years."

High rollers soon moved in for the purpose of using S & L funds for dubious real estate ventures and other such activities, leading in time to the gutting of many financial institutions that the government would later be compelled by law to save. Unfortunately for the many honest investors who lost their money, the Reagan administration, driven by the mistaken belief that markets always know best, failed (or refused) to provide the proper regulatory and administrative oversight that could have prevented this situation from developing into a major financial scandal of such size and scope that Americans would continue to pay for an S & L bailout well into the twenty-first century.

Also, there were major developments on Wall Street and elsewhere that coincided with the new market permissiveness that Reagan ushered in with his victories in 1980 and 1984. The merger mania of the eighties had become a genuine market happening, inspired by go-go hustlers who advanced the proposition that "greed is healthy" and that government regulation and antitrust suits were bad. Helped by the emergence of the junk bond industry, corporate raiders such as T. Boone Pickens and Ivan Boesky became the prototypes of the new entrepreneurs of that decade. Unfortunately for the country, much of their work in amassing new forms of corporate wealth had little or nothing to do with productive investment or business activity designed to produce jobs for American workers and better products for the new global marketplace. Rather, their object was to engage in "corporate raids, takeovers, and leveraged buyouts" in a new predatory environment that was fashioned by such strategically cunning investment bankers as Michael Milken, whose earnings in 1987 alone totaled $550 million. Apropos of Milken's work, as well as others who were similarly employed, humorist Mark Russell remarked that "investment banking has become to productive enterprise in this country what mud wrestling is to the performing arts."

As a result of the constant shuffling and rearranging of assets that characterized the behavior of investment bankers, corporate America, very much like the national government, soon found itself burdened with heavy debt. Hostile takeovers and leveraged buyouts had become the new game in town, helping to ensure that those companies forced to play it would become heavily dependent on borrowed money. The debt load of many corporations soon went through the ceiling, forcing them to pay more than 50 cents of every dollar of pretax earnings in interest on their debt, as compared to 33 cents in the seventies, or 16 cents in the sixties. Given the magnitude of that debt, the Brookings Institution projected that another deep recession, like the one in 1981–82, would bankrupt one out of ten American firms.

While the contours of corporate capitalism changed as a result of these antics on Wall Street, conservatives glowed. Secretary of Education William Bennett boasted that "American conservatism now sets the terms of our debate. It does so because, without in the least abandoning its principles, it has succeeded in identifying with the quintessential American appetite for new challenges and new opportunities." Although Bennett eagerly claimed the high moral and political ground for the conservative movement, that movement began to lose something of its momentum now that certain goals had been reached. As poll data showed, Reagan's tax cuts and successful fight against inflation had gone far to satisfy many Americans, whose mistrust of government was now somewhat diminished. The same data also confirmed that Reagan's massive arms buildup, coupled with his summit meetings with Mikhail Gorbachev, had contributed significantly to the easing of American fears about the Soviet Union.

Ironically, Reagan's domestic achievements engendered a sense of complacency among rank-and-file New Rightists for the first time since he had taken office in 1981. Consequently, the flow of money into New Right coffers slowed considerably, and the organizational zeal that had been its hallmark since the late seventies could no longer be sustained. In fact, Richard Viguerie, direct-mail wizard of the New Right, was not only forced to lay off hundreds of staff people, he ended up selling his magazine, the *Conservative Digest*. The Young Americans for Freedom (YAF), an important youth organization for conservatives, had all but disappeared by the mid-eighties as a result of lost élan and internal corruption. Jerry Falwell's Moral Majority not only was experiencing severe financial problems but was suffering from such public hostility that its name was changed to the Liberty Federation.

Reagan's efforts to establish better relations with the Soviet Union sparked a revolt among many conservatives who were decidedly unhappy with his diplomatic initiatives and clear disavowal of the rhetoric of the "evil empire." For example, Norman Podhoretz, a staunch Reaganite intellectual, felt betrayed by Reagan's actions, charging that his administration was now pursuing "rollover," not "rollback," in its dealings with Moscow. Fantasizing at the top of his creative powers, Podhoretz, according to writer John Judis, went so far as to compare "Gorbachev's Russia with a sanitized Nazi Germany." George Will, a *Newsweek* columnist, also spoke for many aggrieved conservatives and some liberals when he denounced glasnost as nothing more than "a carefully controlled tactic to confuse the West."

Reagan was in an excellent position to ignore such criticism, since he was supported by poll data showing that Americans generally approved his slowly evolving policy of détente with Moscow. Subsequent to his meeting with Mikhail Gorbachev in Iceland, Reagan campaigned across the country in the hope that his participation in the 1986 midterm election would help his party retain its majority in the Senate. He went into twenty-two states imploring voters to give the "Gipper" one more victory. He reminded them of Jimmy Carter's record and defended his own, without offering the country anything new or fresh for the future. Here was a clearly tired president with a shopworn agenda reaching out for support. Although the voters still accepted him, they rejected his message by sending eight new Democratic senators to Washington, including several from the South. As a result of that election, the GOP lost its control of the upper chamber.

Despite a 38 percent turnout of eligible voters, which was the lowest for a midterm election since 1942, the Democrats managed to prevail in 1986 because polarizing issues of culture and race were not so dominant, and because they benefited from the fact that the Reagan prosperity had not actually trickled down to everyone. Vast regions of the country, including the agricultural and industrial Midwest, were decidedly less well off than the booming bicoastal areas. Democrats also scored some much-needed points by calling for new programs to cope with the explosion of drug-related crimes. As the public's attention turned inward to issues that the Democrats could exploit, they received enough votes to capture Congress, suggesting indeed that split-level government was what the country wanted and got.

The Democrats were also lucky to do so well in 1986. The Republicans received a higher percentage of the total votes cast for Senate candidates in 1986 (49 percent) than in 1980 (47 percent), the year they captured the Senate by winning twelve seats. In fact, if there had been a shift of only 26,000 votes to Republican candidates in several closely contested races, they would have retained control of the upper chamber, which had made possible the legislative success of the Reagan Revolution. Having tasted defeat that year, the chief lesson Republicans learned from it was that the politics of polarization—associated with cultural and racial issues—might be the appropriate strategy to follow in the presidential year of 1988.

There was ample evidence to suggest that Democrats were vulnerable to such a campaign. Voter drop-off among one-time strong Democratic identifiers had persisted well into the eighties; that meant the considerable loss of support from lower-middle-class and working-class whites, who had been responding to the politics of conservative egalitarianism as articulated by Republicans ever since the sixties. Those voters saw the GOP as the party of equal opportunity and merit, because it opposed preferential treatment for black Americans and other minority groups. And those same voters saw the Democrats as the champions of affirmative action programs, which had benefited various minorities at their expense. For millions of once-loyal Democrats, that stance had fatally compromised the party's age-old commitment to the principle of economic equality and opportunity for all citizens.

The deepening crisis of the urban underclass, which Thomas and Mary Edsall described as "the Achilles' heel of the liberal movement," also complicated the racial problem for the Democrats. Growing street crime, drug warfare, and an epidemic of teenage pregnancies had convinced many voters across the country that money spent on social welfare programs for the ghetto was wasted on people who simply refused to work. Republicans capitalized on the perceived failure of liberals to address the matter of the disintegrating black family and the often nihilistic behavior of some poor blacks. Much to their long-term political detriment, liberals focused, instead, on racist structures and institutions to justify their support of welfare programs, thereby avoiding a serious discussion of behavioral factors. Moreover, as historian Fred Siegel points out, when liberal Democrats spoke on behalf of civil rights, they thought that they were defending the integrationist vision of Martin Luther King, Jr.; when most whites heard their rhetoric, however, they saw and heard, in the words of Siegel, "Malcolm X or one of his many current legatees, among whom Stokely Carmichael's assertion of twenty years ago has become common fare: 'integration is a subterfuge for the maintenance of white supremacy.'"

Unable to counter the growing racialization of American politics, the Democrats were also hurt by the fact that the AFL-CIO, still an organizational and financial mainstay of their party, was no longer the political force it had been only ten years earlier. Its ranks had been decimated by globalization at a time when it was forced to compete in Congress with well-funded corporate PACs for influence and position. Although labor worked hard in 1986 to win votes for the Democrats, the loss of four million union members since 1975, coupled with the disappearance of two million jobs in manufacturing in the eighties, had left it with far fewer resources with which to mobilize voters on behalf of various progressive causes. Thus, the drift to the GOP by Reagan Democrats, which had become such a prominent feature of the American political landscape since 1980, remained virtually unchallenged by any other element inside the national Democratic party now that the labor movement was on the ropes.

The White House also had problems, which created a serious political roadblock in the immediate aftermath of the 1986 election. The shocking news that President Reagan had traded arms for hostages with Iran, and that funds from those sales to Iran had been diverted to the Contras in Nicaragua, in violation of congressional sanctions, sent his standing in the polls plummeting. A New York Times/CBS poll of December 2, 1986, revealed that he had dropped from 67 percent to 46 percent, representing the sharpest one-month decline in a polling history that went back to 1936. Even worse, the fact that Reagan's White House and the CIA had acted sub rosa to subvert the congressional statute (the Boland Amendment) forbidding the Contras any such assistance opened the door to the possibility that Congress might yet move to impeach the president.

Congress, having initiated impeachment hearings against Richard Nixon, was in no mood to push the case against Reagan for one simple reason: the American people wanted him slapped, not destroyed, for his role in the Iran-Contra affair. After several months of being in virtual limbo as a result of this crisis, Reagan managed to restore his position of authority with a speech to the country on March 4, 1987, in which he acknowledged that the policy of trading arms for hostages was indeed a "mistake." Poll data showed an immediate jump of nine points in his approval rating, leaving him now at 51 percent. Reagan's subsequent dealings with Gorbachev kept him busy and at the center of events, but never again would he be the totally trusted "magical Sun King" of American politics or "the Prospero of American memories," in Lou Cannon's words.

The results of the 1986 election, plus the Iran-Contra affair, had unquestionably weakened the Republicans. Their stand on certain issues no longer ran parallel with the mood of the country. Poll data suggested in 1987 that the American people were now willing to look more favorably at the return of a more activist government to deal with such matters as the environment: 61 percent wanted more regulation, and only 6 percent wanted less. At the same time, public opinion had also shifted dramatically on the question as to whether there was too much government regulation of the economy: in 1980, 67 percent answered yes; by 1987, only 38 percent did. Such data went far to confirm the view of one student of regulatory politics that by 1987 "the anti-government revolt of the 1970s [was] over."

With that shift in the public's mood, and their own victory in 1986, Democrats thought that they might yet capture the presidency in 1988. Some observers, such as James Reichley, even thought that as a result of the 1986 election a post-Reagan political era had begun. After all, the Reagan agenda was spent, and the president himself seemed to be out of touch. Yet, Republicans had to be comforted by poll data showing that many more Americans agreed than disagreed that the GOP could be far better trusted to produce prosperity and to cut inflation than could the Democrats. Although more Americans wanted an activist government to protect their physical environment and their health and safety in the workplace and to help improve their schools, they still did not want that same government pushing affirmative action programs down their throats or spending what they considered wasted tax dollars on the black underclass. Happily for the Republicans, their racial politics and policies coincided with the national outlook on these matters, thereby ensuring that they would take a politically popular stand during any debate on regulatory issues affecting race and rights during the presidential campaign of 1988.

Besides having the economy working in its favor, the GOP also retained a solid presidential stronghold in the South. There, its position had been considerably augmented by the New Religious Right, which had responded enthusiastically to the party's stand on race and religion. Adding millions of new voters to the Republican rolls, the religious right helped provide the GOP with a seemingly secure lock on the 138 electoral votes represented by the states of the old Confederacy, as well as with another strong conservative base located in the Rocky Mountains and Sunbelt West.

Beginning with the primaries and extending into the convention itself, the religious right was now an important part of the nominating process inside the Republican party. Having a position somewhat comparable to that of organized labor inside the Democratic party, the religious right represented about 15 to 20 percent of all delegates to that Republican convention, so it was in a good position not only to exert pressure on various candidates but to extract concessions from them in exchange for its support.

Vice-President George Bush, a graduate of Andover Academy and Yale University and whose family's roots ran deep into the old eastern Republican establishment, worked hard to line up support from that bloc. As a Reagan loyalist, he had long since moved away from previously held positions, such as supporting a woman's right to an abortion or opposing prayer in the public schools, which would have placed him on ideological grounds unacceptable to the religious right. In addition to repudiating seemingly once firm beliefs, Bush eagerly courted Jim Bakker, the televangelist who would later be involved in a major scandal affecting the operations of his Praise The Lord (PTL) organization. And he obtained a useful endorsement from Jerry Falwell, at a time when Pat Robertson, a Falwell rival and fellow televangelist, was thinking about making a run for the Republican presidential nomination in 1988. But Bush had already beaten him and other putative candidates to the punch: supported by the regular Republican organizations in the South, as well as by a number of important officials on the religious right, he had established a strong regional base with which to strengthen his bid for the Republican nomination many months before the primary season had even begun.

While Bush consolidated his position in the face of a surefire challenge from other Republicans, the administration was busily trying to secure the Senate's confirmation of Judge Robert Bork for a seat on the Supreme Court. An outspoken proponent of a conservative legal philosophy predicated on the theory of original intent, Bork lost his bid to join the Court after the Senate rejected his nomination in October 1987. Even though the Reagan administration lost this particular battle, it was still winning the judicial war. Judge Anthony Kennedy, an unobtrusive conservative jurist, was later nominated in

Bork's stead, and he was quickly confirmed by the Senate to fill the vacancy on the high court. By the time Reagan left the presidency, he had put his stamp not only on the Supreme Court but on the entire federal judiciary, to the extent that over half of the sitting judges had received their appointments from him. Here, then, on one level was the heart and soul of the Reagan Revolution: the judiciary, including a narrow majority on the Supreme Court, had been captured, so to speak, for the purpose of dramatically narrowing, if not repudiating, the "rights revolution," which had been nurtured and institutionalized earlier by both the Warren and the Burger courts. That powerful conservative challenge to their libertarian precedents would be particularly noticeable in the area of criminal law and individual rights of the accused. In the event the Supreme Court later moved to reverse or undercut past decisions protecting a woman's reproductive rights or affirmative action programs, it would legally validate an important part of the cultural and political agenda of the Reagan coalition, which was otherwise not obtainable through the legislative process via Congress. (Ironically, the "rights revolution," which conservatives had been denouncing for years, was itself driven largely by judicial fiat, and only occasionally by action taken by Congress.)

Meanwhile, there were other developments to suggest that American capitalism could still produce surprises. On October 19, 1987, the New York stock market dropped by over 500 points, which was the biggest single one-day decline in the market's history. Although the causes for that sudden nosedive were complex, tied as they were to technical operations and to the convergence of domestic and international market forces, short-term shock waves immediately rippled throughout the entire global financial system. Thanks to quick intervention by the Federal Reserve Board, which guaranteed the necessary liquidity to keep business and financial operations running smoothly, buyer confidence in the market was quickly restored. Prices for stock shares soon began to climb once more, suggesting to some observers that one such extraordinary day of panic selling represented only a mere blip on the economic screen and was not in itself a cause for deep concern.

The spectacular size and continuing growth of the federal deficit, along with the vast imbalance in the country's international trade account, were far more worrisome for many in the business community. Peter Peterson, once Richard Nixon's secretary of commerce and now an important and respected Wall Street figure, spoke for them when he expressed the starkly un-Reaganite view that the American economy was now in deep trouble as a result of that debt load. Peterson claimed that a "consumption bacchanalia," generated by the enormous deficit of the eighties, had been responsible for creating many of the problems currently affecting the economy. In order to augment or bolster a diminished savings rate that had been wasted in a flood of personal consumption, he argued that a major austerity program was required so that a more solid foundation could be placed under America's financial house. Peterson, therefore, recommended ending the universality of nonmeans-tested entitlement programs such as Social Security, cutting labor costs, and reducing living standards in order to help lessen the country's dependence on foreign funds and to build up sufficient equity in domestic capital markets. He believed that if such bitter medicine were taken now, it would go far to restore America's position as a first-class competitor in world markets.

That so-called consumption bacchanalia notwithstanding, the massive increase in military spending in the Reagan years, coupled with the vaunted Reagan tax cuts of 1981 and 1986, had been primarily responsible for producing the huge deficit that Peterson currently deplored. If he correctly saw that the heavy indebtedness of the American economy was indeed a serious problem, his proposed solutions for coping with the legacy of Reaganomics, if acted upon, would have gone far to dismantle the country's already limited welfare state.

Although corporate executives had reason to worry about the macroeconomic consequences of Reaganomics, they personally benefited from it. Many who signed Peterson's advertisement for a "bipartisan budget appeal," which appeared in the *New York Times* on November 9, 1987, "could see," in Kevin Phillips's words, "the favorable side of the loose fiscal equation: the attractiveness of low tax brackets and high real interest rates for maid-and-chauffeur precincts like Sutton Place, Round Hill Road, and Bel Air. In dollars banked, consumed, or couponed between 1981 and 1988, the amounts involved were massive."

Democrats were caught in the web of fiscal restraint at a time when Republican "heyday" economics validated the principle that those who have, get. Afraid either to raise taxes or increase the deficit, they helped to pass both versions of the Gramm-Rudman-Hollings Bill, which imposed mandatory budget cuts on many do-

mestic programs that their core constituents needed. As a further indication of their political futility, New York governor Mario Cuomo,
a luminary in the Democratic New Deal tradition, had gone so far as
to escort Peterson around Washington in late 1987 and had endorsed
his plan for the creation of a bipartisan budget commission that
would seek to impose tight controls over the budgetary process with
the aim of achieving a balanced budget.

Even though poll data suggested that the country was now in-
clined to support a more active federal government than at any time
since the beginning of the Reagan era, Democrats, going into the
1988 election, still lacked an agenda that truly separated them from
traditional GOP budget balancers. At least they had the satisfaction
of knowing that the Republican presidential nominee this time
would not be Ronald Reagan. Yet, potential Democratic candidates
carried with them the baggage of a racial liberalism that had not
worn well with many American voters since the sixties. Moreover,
what could they say that would interest the average American voter
in a period of peace and relative prosperity, or in the aftermath of
Ronald Reagan's triumph over inflation and the remarkable Interme-
diate Nuclear Force (INF) treaty he had negotiated with Mikhail Gorbachev?

For a majority of Americans, that prosperity still had substance.
Despite the fact that real wages had stagnated since the early seventies, unemployment had already dropped below 6 percent at the end
of 1987 and the utilization of existing plant capacity had climbed
above 80 percent. It seemed from all outward appearances, then, that
the larger economy was now well positioned to achieve at least 4 percent real growth in 1988. If that happened, the voters would surely
give the GOP credit for its responsible economic stewardship. The
Democrats, in the meantime, would be deprived of the one key issue
they needed, above all, to capture the White House in 1988.

Among the several Democratic presidential candidates, only
Congressman Richard Gephardt and the Reverend Jesse Jackson had
anything significant to say about the economy. Gephardt, focusing
attention on the large trade deficit incurred during the Reagan years,
championed the cause of economic nationalism and endorsed trade
protectionism as the best way to cope with the surge of foreign imports into American markets. His proposal for action, designed to
protect domestic jobs and markets from excessive foreign competition, offered a well-defined alternative to the free-market, laissez-

faire approach to international trade, which had largely characterized the Reagan administration's policies and behavior since 1981. Gephardt's campaign for the presidency sputtered in New Hampshire and later died in Michigan, but his initiative raised the hackles and fears of free traders in both parties, including Governor Michael Dukakis of Massachusetts, another Democratic presidential candidate. Dukakis, speaking for many exporters and importers, was clearly afraid that Gephardt's approach would greatly exacerbate already tense trade relations between Japan and the United States.

Jackson's attack on the process of globalization was far more radical and wide-ranging than Gephardt's. He denounced the power and economic transactions of the multinational corporations, charging them with having a greater interest in "green, green, green" than "red, white, and blue." And he sought to mobilize support via his Rainbow Coalition for those most hurt by Reaganomics and globalization, including the ghetto poor and those many millions who were now trapped inside the minimum wage economy. As in 1984, he called, among other things, for massive federal spending directed at creating jobs, a national health insurance program, and increased taxes on the wealthy beneficiaries of the 1981 tax cut. And he also proposed major cuts in the military budget, arguing that the cold war had ended.

Unfortunately for Jackson, his was a political and social agenda on behalf of left-liberalism that a majority of Democrats were not prepared to support privately, much less debate publicly. Though he did well by winning several primaries in the South on Super Tuesday, and triumphed in the Michigan primary, Jackson had taken his own campaign for racial and social justice in America to its outermost political limits. In an effort to expand his Rainbow Coalition significantly beyond its already narrow class and racial base of 1984, Jackson had failed to attract a sufficient number of white voters—other than some upper-middle-class ex-McGovernites. But he was never truly a serious prospect in the minds of most Democrats, for reasons having to do with his race, personality, and program. Yet if Jackson was running in order to become "president of black America," as Sidney Blumenthal has suggested, he also managed, with great resolve, to dramatize those political issues and economic concerns that few others in the Democratic party were prepared to confront in 1988. Nevertheless, after having lost the fight for the nomination, he would not willingly leave the spotlight; he soon emerged as a political millstone around the neck of the party's eventual nominee, Michael Dukakis, by alienating many voters who wanted nothing to do with a party that had him as a major spokesman.

Dukakis successfully made his way through the Democratic primary maze without a serious mishap. Helped by the political demise of front-running Gary Hart, resulting from adverse publicity concerning his sexual liaisons, and supported by vastly better funding than the other candidates, he had virtually locked up the nomination by the late spring of 1988 with his "themeless" campaign. And with Democratic presidential prospects on the upswing, Dukakis was prepared to take a united party into the fall campaign.

Despite the recent shift in the national mood that opened the possibility for new departures, Dukakis himself was no ardent proponent of change. He believed, instead, in the importance of bringing good management techniques to government by stressing competence over ideology; in short, he would not confront, let alone seriously discuss, many of the key domestic problems and issues that Jesse Jackson and Richard Gephardt had raised during their run for the nomination. Dukakis, like Jimmy Carter before him, was as much concerned with the process as the results that were achieved. He saw the administrative trees, not the ideological forest.

But Dukakis was more than just another technocratic politician with good connections at the Kennedy School of Government at Harvard University. He was also a liberal of a certain legal bent and cast of mind, whose values and views made it possible, later, for the GOP to cook him for dinner. A proud member of the American Civil Liberties Union, he believed in the necessity of protecting, in journalist Harold Myerson's words, "the one against the many—*not the many against the powerful.*" Dukakis's brand of liberalism, which had its roots in the decisions taken by the Warren and Burger courts of the sixties and seventies, did not embrace the class politics associated with Franklin Roosevelt or renew the social contract in Jesse Jackson's terms. Rather, it was identified with those cosmopolitan cultural values and beliefs that were best expressed in a highly legalistic context that had been shaped by such Supreme Court decisions as *Roe v. Wade.* Consequently, large numbers of Americans, worried about the breakdown of the criminal justice system or concerned about the impact of affirmative action programs on their family's future, found the elitist "liberalism" of the Dukakis variety a threat to their sense of traditional morality and fair play.

Before the Republicans could expose and exploit that side of Dukakis, they first had to settle their own business of selecting a nominee to succeed Ronald Reagan. Although George Bush had been the front runner, he had been badly hurt by coming in third in the Iowa caucuses behind Senator Bob Dole and the Reverend Pat Robertson. But he saved his sagging campaign in New Hampshire, where help provided by Governor John Sununu and Reagan loyalists made it possible for him to dispatch Dole, his archrival. Bush later wrapped up matters with big wins in the South and the West, putting to rest any residual challenge coming from Robertson, who, along with Congressman Jack Kemp, had assisted him earlier by splitting the vote on the Republican right. Thus, Bush had won the fight for the nomination by pledging, as he did in New Hampshire, not to raise taxes; by shrewdly courting the right in 1986 and 1987 with his stand on abortion and prayer in the public schools; and, above all, by benefiting from his close working relationship with the ever-popular Ronald Reagan.

Although Bush had a reasonably productive economy working for him in the summer of 1988, he was still in deep trouble because Dukakis came out of the July Democratic convention with a seven teen-point lead in the polls. Faced with that reality, plus the difficult task of trying to define himself to the voters, Bush knew that he had a serious problem now that the steam had gone out of the conservative movement. Seeking a role to play, he was prepared to function as a consolidator, not an innovator, saying, "We don't need radical new directions—we need strong and steady leadership. We don't need to remake society—we just need to remember who we are." Bush also remembered, far better than Dukakis, that "ideology is important."

Pursuant to that point, Bush and his key advisers, led by Lee Atwater, focused on an aspect of Dukakis's politics and values that they thought could be turned to their advantage. They were no doubt aware that he had been successfully savaged in 1978 by the culturally and politically conservative Ed King in their primary race for governor of Massachusetts, a race that Dukakis, the incumbent, lost in part because of his liberal views on abortion and capital punishment. They also knew that in the 1982 primary election Dukakis, running once more against King, had lost a fifty-six point lead in the polls, winning by a margin of only 8 percent. Although Dukakis managed to defeat King, whose administration had been riddled with corruption, his inability to attract or to hold the support of blue-collar ethnic voters had been exposed for a second time in as many elections.

Bush and his campaign staff used that material about Dukakis's past as the basis for their focus group interviews; they found that the voters were irate about the Willie Horton case as well as Dukakis's stand on the Pledge of Allegiance. Here was precisely what they needed to hammer home the point that Dukakis was just another "liberal" and that he was more concerned with protecting the rights of minorities and special interest groups than in safeguarding those mainstream cultural values shared by a majority of Americans.

The Willie Horton case was especially lethal because it concerned a black felon who, although he had been imprisoned for having committed murder, was given under Massachusetts penal statutes the right to weekend furloughs. While out on his tenth weekend pass, he raped a white woman and physically assaulted her fiancé. Later captured and jailed in the state of Maryland, Horton soon became a national cause célèbre, focusing attention on the rules and procedures governing the release or the furlough of prisoners convicted of murder in the state of Massachusetts.

Although the legislation that had made Horton's furlough possible was passed during the administration of a Republican predecessor, Dukakis opposed all efforts to change it. In 1976 he vetoed, in the name of a prisoner rehabilitation program, a bill that would have denied convicts such as Horton a pass that the current law still authorized. Dukakis never offered an apology or even expressed his regrets to the two individuals who had been subjected to Horton's violent attack, thereby lending credence to Bush's charge that the Massachusetts governor was not only an "ice man" but was also soft on crime.

Coupled with the Horton affair, with all of its harsh and ugly racial and sexual overtones, was the matter of the Pledge of Allegiance. Dukakis was also open to the charge that he was a rights-minded liberal who was indifferent to other vastly more important national values. He had vetoed a state bill requiring teachers to lead their students in the Pledge of Allegiance on the grounds that the Supreme Court many years earlier had clearly stated that any person who refused to say it was legally entitled not to do so. Although Dukakis's veto was constitutionally and legally correct, it offended many people who felt that his action was decidedly unpatriotic. And along with the Horton affair, it provided Lee Atwater with the symbolic material he needed to overcome Dukakis's big lead in the polls.

Bush quickly forged to the front once Dukakis's position on both issues was revealed to the public via a Republican media blitz. Thanks, then, to Atwater's game plan, Bush was able to stage one of the most remarkable comebacks in American political history. By Labor Day, his lead over Dukakis was so solid that he seemed a sure bet to become Ronald Reagan's successor. Despite the fact that he had alarmed many people by selecting a conservative lightweight, Senator Dan Quayle of Indiana, to be his running mate, Bush's choice cost him no significant loss of support from those voters who felt the race for the presidency was what mattered and who were prepared to leave the rest for the pundits to discuss and debate.

Bush's standing was further enhanced by good news on the economic front. By September, voters were very upbeat about their current situation, feeling with good reason that they were far better off than they had been at the beginning of the Reagan era. Growth was averaging 4.5 percent for the year, unemployment now stood at 5.6 percent, inflation was no worse than 4 percent, millions of new jobs had been created, and the longest sustained period of peacetime prosperity in the nation's history had not yet run out of fuel.

Nor was there any diminution in the country's warm feelings for President Reagan, who now stood at 60 percent in the opinion polls. His popularity had once again zoomed upward because the economy was good, because voters warmly supported his policy of détente and cooperation with Mikhail Gorbachev, and, also, because a majority of Americans liked him. That recent upsurge for Reagan, coming when it did, clearly translated into votes for Bush, whose election was seen by many as akin to giving a third term to Reagan.

With just over 50 percent of eligible voters turning out to cast their ballots, Bush won the election, receiving nearly 54 percent of the vote and a big sweep in the electoral college. Yet, his victory was not as overwhelming as it might have seemed. His percentage of the total votes cast was below Reagan's 59 percent of 1984. Also, support from a key bloc of younger voters between the ages of 18 and 29 had dropped from 59 percent in 1984 to 52 percent in 1988. Women voters, significantly, gave him only one more percentage point than they gave to Dukakis, which was far less than their male counterparts gave to Bush. And, to the dismay of congressional Republicans, Bush's coattails were nonexistent, since the Democrats won two additional seats in the House and picked up one more in the Senate.

That Dukakis may have blown an opportunity by conducting an

inept and mediocre campaign is confirmed by the fact that he made real gains in the last two weeks before the election after telling working-class voters that he was on their side. By that time, however, it was already far too late for him to make up the ground lost to Bush back in August and September, at a time when millions of voters had already been exposed to the Horton advertisements and informed about his stand on the Pledge of Allegiance. Yet he still won ten states and came fairly close in others, including California and Illinois. Moreover, he received a greater percentage of the votes cast than had either Jimmy Carter or Walter Mondale when they ran against Ronald Reagan, or had Hubert Humphrey or George McGovern when they challenged Richard Nixon. In fact, if there had been a shift of about 535,000 votes in eleven key states won by Bush, Dukakis would have won a narrow victory via the electoral college.

Dukakis's basic problem was one that had been plaguing the Democrats for years. He lacked the votes to win because the Democratic core had been steadily shrinking ever since the sixties as a result of racial and cultural conflict, higher taxes, and globalization. By late 1988, only 37 percent of the voters were willing to identify themselves as Democrats, compared to 43 percent in 1980 and 53 percent in 1964. GOP identifiers in 1988 were just a shade behind the Democrats, with 34 percent, but when a large bloc of independents, residing in suburban America, was included in the count, the Republicans still had a solid working majority operating in their favor on the level of presidential politics.

As a result of this election, the Democrats added to their majority in Congress; their victory, however, was really a massive triumph for incumbency, having been underwritten by a heavy infusion of PAC money amounting to $31.7 million from corporations and trade associations and less than $24 million from unions. So while the Democratic party successfully protected its turf in Congress with the help of corporate money, it did not offer enough to attract those lower-middle-class and working-class Americans whose votes in a presidential year were often determined by their racial and cultural views. In order to reach those voters, Democrats would first have to escape from the deficit trap that Ronald Reagan had so cleverly sprung on them in the early eighties, which George Bush had reinforced with his campaign pledge of no new taxes.

While Bush was preparing to move into the White House, Ronald Reagan gave his farewell address to the American people. Reagan talked about the various changes he had helped to bring about, saying, "They called it the Reagan Revolution, and I'll accept that, but for me it always seemed like the Great Discovery: a discovery of our values and common sense." On one level, Reagan was correct. He took a disillusioned nation, burdened with the memory of Vietnam, shocked by the scandal of Watergate, and caught in the coils of stagflation and global market changes, and gave it a short-term rhetorical lift via reillusionment. Motivated by imperial nostalgia abroad and ambivalence about the role of the state at home, Americans were receptive to Reagan's message, not just because it was orchestrated with great panache and telegenic style, but because it reaffirmed at precisely the right time a longstanding American suspicion of government, hatred of taxes, and love of country.

But the Reagan Revolution went well beyond the rediscovery or reaffirmation of the old faith. Reagan's powerful presence and personal appeal moved the national political agenda to the right on virtually every significant issue of the day: taxes, regulation, military spending, affirmative action, abortion rights, and environmentalism. Having won the ideological battle, he had made it very difficult for liberal Democrats to convince the public that the time was right for the restoration of an activist government, which would promote the social programs they wanted or thought the country needed.

Senator Edward Kennedy understood precisely what Reagan had wrought. Speaking at Yale University shortly after Reagan left office, he declared: "Whether we agree with him or not, Ronald Reagan was a successful candidate and an effective president above all else because he stood for a set of ideas. He stated them in 1980—and it turned out that he meant them—and he wrote most of them not only into public law but into the national consciousness." According to Kennedy, "Ronald Reagan may have forgotten names but never his goals. He was a great communicator, not simply because of his personality or his TelePrompTer, but mostly because he had something to communicate."

At the same time that Kennedy praised Reagan, he also attacked Michael Dukakis for having run a campaign in which "ideology was missing." Taking the strongest exception to Dukakis's claim that the campaign was about competence, Kennedy said that such a tack allowed George Bush to win the election by filling the Democratic void "with appeals to fear, only lightly sprinkled with the kinder, gentler seasoning of his perorations."

Such "seasoning" notwithstanding, Bush took office on January 20, 1989, declaring that as a result of the huge deficit now confronting him he had more "will than wallet." Unlike Reagan, then, he was not prepared to break new ground, and he had no clearly defined domestic agenda to offer the country. Whether this would allow him to preserve Republican hegemony or would open the door to a liberal revival depended very much on the state of the national economy and on how he exercised leadership during the four years he was scheduled to serve as president of the United States.

During President Bush's first few months in office, the economy grew at an average annual rate of 3.5 percent and unemployment stood at 5.3 percent. Since Bush's major interest lay in foreign affairs, the continuing good news from the home front provided him with an opportunity for exploring new ways of dealing with Moscow now that the cold war appeared to be over.

Bush's position during the 1988 campaign was somewhat to the right of Ronald Reagan's, as he warned the country about the need to remain vigilant about the Soviet threat despite the success of the INF treaty and the promising beginning of the strategic arms limitation talks. Even after taking office, he moved slowly vis-à-vis Moscow. For instance, he was not yet willing to go as far as Reagan in saying that the cold war was over; nor did he favor faster progress on behalf of a strategic arms control agreement, which his predecessor had eagerly promoted, without first engaging in a prolonged "strategic review." But after Mikhail Gorbachev refused to use force to put down nationalist (anti-Soviet) upheavals in Eastern Europe and did not oppose the reunification of Germany, the European situation was historically transformed. Consequently, those events pushed Bush in the direction of a far more accommodating relationship with Gorbachev and the Soviet Union. After giving Gorbachev full credit for helping to end the cold war, Bush was forced to admit that indeed times had changed.

Even conservatives, who knew that anticommunism had been the glue that had held their coalition together for so long, recognized that this was a transcendent historical moment. But if the rollback of communism had been their goal even before the Goldwater era, the containment of communism had also dominated the politics of the liberal center ever since the late forties. Thus, for more than a generation a gut-wrenching battle had taken place on the contested terrain of American politics with regard to the key question as to how best to fight the cold war.

Suddenly, in 1989–90, many liberals and even some conservatives began to sense that as a result of changed circumstances in Europe a new and different political agenda was needed in order to cope with the pressing geo-economic realities of the nineties. More and more people, led by liberal economist Robert Kuttner and Reagan administration trade negotiator Clyde Prestowitz, asked probing questions about the state of the American economy, reflecting a growing national concern about the daunting Japanese and German challenge to America's economic hegemony and leadership. At the same time, a majority of citizens also welcomed the opportunity to use a prospective "peace dividend," produced by the ending of the cold war, to confront a variety of domestic needs, including the plight of the homeless and the spread of the drug culture.

The growing anxiety about the current economic and social state of affairs was captured well by the Business Roundtable, the voice of America's corporate elite. Hoping to encourage governmental action to reduce the deficit, it released a statement in April 1990 that clearly stated the price the country had paid for its eighties binge. "In the brief period of the past decade, we have amassed trillions of dollars of debt; we have regressed from being the largest creditor nation in the world to the biggest debtor; we have witnessed the federal deficit absorb over half our net private savings; we have become increasingly dependent upon foreign capital, inexorably ceding our influence over both our domestic and international policies. And we have embarked upon a course which cannot be sustained without high cost—economic and social and human." Although the Business Roundtable provided a telling commentary on the budgetary and fiscal policies of the Reagan administration, it neatly sidestepped any discussion of how much corporate America had also benefited from the antilabor, antiregulatory, low-tax, promarket policies of that administration, whose rich legacy of economic contradictions would soon encumber the Bush White House.

While deficit reduction was high on Bush's agenda, he was also absorbed with other domestic issues in 1989, such as a war on drugs and an amendment to the Constitution concerning flag burning. After the Supreme Court declared in a 5-4 decision that flag burning was a form of symbolic speech which was protected by the First

Amendment, President Bush—eager to placate cultural conservatives—called for a constitutional amendment to prohibit any such desecration of the Stars and Stripes. With that action, he placed the congressional Democrats in a bind until they were able to pass legislation in early October to protect the flag and thereby avoid a bruising battle over the amending process.

Bush's action in this regard was hardly surprising. He was intent on safeguarding his position with the Republican right, which had become the dominant bloc inside the party. The flag issue thus allowed him to keep his lines of communication open to the right wing and to demonstrate a sensitivity to its concerns. Meanwhile, the conservative position on a variety of issues, from the flag amendment to abortion, was well defended inside the administration by such ideological stalwarts of the right as Vice-President Dan Quayle, Secretary of Housing and Urban Development Jack Kemp, and White House Chief of Staff John Sununu.

Bush also declared war on drugs, appointing William Bennett, a former Reagan cabinet officer, to lead the fight against this national scourge. But the money that the administration requested and received from Congress for its campaign was hopelessly insufficient, since the problem of drugs had become a widespread plague, especially in the inner cities of the country. In time, that drug war, designed to produce a quick political fix for the White House, faded from view, as other problems associated with a souring American economy eventually superseded it.

Bush's drug war, coupled with his conservative social agenda, did not help Republican candidates win office in 1989. Douglas Wilder, a black Democrat, was elected governor of Virginia with the help of upscale Republican women from the Washington suburbs, who rallied to him because of his pro-choice stand on abortion rights. Democrat James Florio, running hard as a pro-choice candidate, was elected governor of New Jersey, defeating an opponent who had embraced the position of the many pro-lifers. The Supreme Court's recent decision in the case of *Webster v. Reproductive Services of Missouri*, which gave the states more power to define the terms of abortion, had evidently scared many libertarian voters into voting for Democratic candidates who were willing to defend *Roe v. Wade*.

Could it be that those results pointed to the possible exhaustion of such a volatile social issue as abortion, which Ronald Reagan and George Bush had exploited so successfully in their respective campaigns to win the presidency? Kevin Phillips thought that the Republican domestic agenda, which included not only abortion but "flag, crime, and taxes," was in danger of becoming "stale," thereby opening the door for the Democrats in 1990. Vice-President Dan Quayle agreed with him, remarking shortly after the election that the GOP needed "a new message," one that dealt with social problems "without resurrecting big government."

During the 1988 campaign, George Bush, in his "kinder, gentler" incarnation, recognized that there were social problems requiring attention, particularly in the area of public education and the environment. But there was little that either he or Congress could or would do to advance even this limited social agenda beyond the point of rhetorical good will, or even very limited additional funding. Democrats refused to support a tax hike without Bush's blessing in advance, and both sides continued to accept the institutional constraints of the Gramm-Rudman-Hollings Act.

While the Republican White House and the Democratic Congress continued to play their symbolic games with the deficit, the beginnings of an economic slowdown finally seemed to be at hand, as was evidenced by the lack of solid growth during the third and fourth quarters of 1989 and the first two quarters of 1990. So while George Bush stood at 70 percent in the opinion polls, the economic concerns of a majority of working Americans began to grow, with 60 percent opining in late 1989 that the country's economic state was "not so good" or "poor." In addition, 64 percent voiced fears that American corporations would be dominated by "foreigners" within a decade.

That many Americans experienced difficulties in coping with the changing economic conditions happened to coincide with the Reagan boom, which had gone far to enhance the positions of the haves while leaving many others on the sidelines. According to economist Mark Levinson, the income of the bottom 20 percent had fallen 6 percent during the decade of the eighties, and income shares of the next 60 percent were now lower than any time since 1947. But at the same time, the income of the top 20 percent had risen 16.7 percent, receiving the highest proportion of income shares ever recorded. While this redistribution of income and wealth was occurring, the total debt of the country, including governmental, corporate, and personal debt, had jumped from $4 trillion at the beginning of the decade to over $11 trillion at the end, placing an enormous financial burden on those who would ultimately have to pay the interest on it.

Statistics also revealed that 13.5 percent of the population in 1990, or 33.6 million Americans, lived in poverty, and that one out of every five children in America was trapped in that same miserable environment. Yet, substantial number of Americans—having already witnessed the failure of other programs to raise people from poverty—were opposed to spending more tax dollars on government programs that appeared to do little good or that did not directly benefit them. They opposed welfarism because of their belief that the inner cities of America were inhabited by irresponsible people who refused to work, engaged in violent crime, and cared little, or not at all, that nearly two-thirds of all African American babies were born out of wedlock.

In the meantime, Democrats had driven many working-class whites from their party as a result of the party's longstanding support for affirmative action and poverty programs. Yet those same Democratic politicians refused to engage in the kind of class politics that might have provided them with a way out of the racial and cultural cul-de-sac in which they found themselves. Lacking such an orientation, they found it hard to politicize the fact that the tax load weighed most heavily on those Americans making between $20,000 and $60,000 a year. So it is not surprising that when Senator Daniel Moynihan proposed in late 1989 to roll back the regressive Social Security tax from 7.51 percent to 6.06 percent, he found little support for his initiative from his own Democratic congressional colleagues. They were far more concerned with the goals of deficit reduction than with either the unfairness of that payroll tax or the need to rethink the purpose and function of the Gramm-Rudman-Hollings Act.

Because of the increase in the Social Security tax in 1983, revenues from that source had increased by 23 percent, allowing the federal government to take in a projected $100 billion more by 1993 than it would have to pay out in benefits; it was further estimated that the Social Security trust fund would exceed $250 billion by the year 2000. Yet few Americans knew or understood that, when their employers' contributions were factored in, their Social Security taxes were higher than their income taxes. Instead, they wanted their income taxes reduced, not the more onerous payroll tax, which was the basis on which each working generation funded the retirement of the older generation. Yet, that older generation had largely climbed out of poverty (the proportion of elderly living below the poverty line dropped from 28.5 percent in 1966 to 12.2 percent in 1987) because of

the Social Security program and the cost of living allowances attached to it, which the Nixon administration had approved virtually
on the eve of the 1972 election.

At the same time Social Security taxes were on the rise, so were
state and local taxes, which had increased from 11 percent of the
GNP in 1980 to 12.2 percent in 1990. In 1981, for example, 36 percent of public services in America were paid for by state and local
taxes; by 1990, that figure stood at 42 percent, coming at a time
when states and municipalities were under intense financial pressure
to pay for increasing demands for much-needed services such as
policing and public health programs. Unlike the national government, many state and local jurisdictions were compelled by law to
balance their budgets, thereby creating the basis for the fiscal crisis
that soon enveloped statehouses from Albany to Sacramento.

That crisis was directly attributable to the policies of Ronald
Reagan. Seizing the opportunity that came with his election in 1980,
he sought to downsize and reduce the responsibilities of the federal
government. Thus, unlike Richard Nixon, Gerald Ford, or Jimmy
Carter, who supported the welfare state via decentralized revenue
sharing with the states and municipalities, he cut back payments to
them. Consequently, in the guise of a Reagan-style "New Federalism," federal aid to the states and municipalities, noted Carol
O'Cleireacain, *"fell by $34 billion in real terms during the decade of
the eighties."* A particularly important development, it forced a considerable number of those jurisdictions into an either-or position; either they had to raise taxes or they had to reduce, or even abolish,
those many social programs and services that the public wanted but
that Reagan now refused to fund or support.

After 1984, Congress began to struggle with its own deficit problem. As a result of the massive debt Reagan had incurred, it sought to
impose a sense of discipline on the budgetary process via the
Gramm-Rudman-Hollings Act, which was designed to force compliance with a balanced budget objective by 1993. Much to the consternation of George Bush, that bill came due in 1990, as the budget
deficit for fiscal year 1991 was a projected $80 billion above the tar-
get goal of a $64 billion deficit. Both he and Congress now faced the
ominous prospect of a shutdown of the government unless both sides
could find a way around the harsh and relentless demands of GRH.

In mid-1990, Bush was forced to make a deal with Congress either to sidestep GRH or to accept the responsibility for seeing many

government programs go into the dumpster. Thus, in order to get the cap on discretionary spending that he wanted while avoiding a curtailment of basic services, he did what he had promised not to do in 1988—he accepted a tax hike. No longer in a position to say, "Read my lips: No new taxes," Bush issued a statement on June 26, 1990, declaring: "It is clear to me that both the size of the deficit problem and the need for a package that can be enacted require all of the following: entitlement and mandatory program reform; tax revenue increases; growth incentives; discretionary spending reductions." Caught in the coils of GRH, Bush had no choice but to play the game. By proposing a tax hike, he alienated his own right wing and revealed the ideological vacuity of the House Democratic leadership. As the great conservative economist Joseph Schumpeter wrote many years earlier, "Public finances are one of the best starting points for an investigation of society, especially though not exclusively of its political life."

The Budget Reconciliation Act (BRA) of 1990 passed through several stages before it finally became law. First came the deal cooked up by the White House and the congressional Democratic leadership, which proposed higher taxes on gasoline, beer, and tobacco, as well as an increase in contributions from individuals eligible for Medicare. This agreement was later voided in the House by a coalition of liberal Democrats and conservative Republicans who objected to its terms and voted it down on October 4, 1990. Those Democrats opposed the deal because it imposed a heavier burden on middle-income Americans than on the wealthy; many Republicans, led by Georgia congressman Newt Gingrich, rejected on grounds of principle and smart political tactics any deal that called for a tax hike.

After the White House and Congress finally reconciled their differences, GRH was replaced by the BRA. Under its terms, the deficit was to be reduced to one percent of the GNP by 1995, and a planned $500 billion reduction in spending was scheduled to take place over a five-year period. In addition, Americans in higher income brackets would have their taxes raised ever so slightly, and the increases in consumption taxes proposed earlier would be somewhat reduced, suggesting that a token element of progressivity had been included in the new agreement. Accordingly, the agreed-upon tax increase would produce $20 billion in new revenues in 1991 and a total of $146 billion over a five-year span.

Most significantly, the BRA was also designed to curtail spending in such a way that from fiscal year 1991 through 1993 no new monies could be added to any particular domestic program without first cutting the same amount from other domestic programs. Only Social Security, debt repayment, and deposit insurance were left untouched by this requirement. The law also stated that funds taken from the military budget could be used only for the purpose of deficit reduction, not for domestic sector programs. If, on the other hand, the president and Congress together agreed that fresh appropriations were needed for a particular program, then new spending would not entail a matching cut from somewhere else in the domestic budget.

President Bush was badly hurt by his commitment to a tax hike, even though he claimed that it was no more than a one-time event. He dropped in the polls as a result of that action, and the GOP suffered about a 10 percent loss among those who had identified themselves as Republicans. It was all very predictable: opposition to tax hikes and support for tax cuts had been central to the supply-side gospel that went into the making of the Reagan coalition. Thus, the anger of conservatives, who had a vested interest in preserving what they thought was the key to their political success in the eighties, was no surprise .

If Bush had given Republican supply-siders cause for ideological angst, his effort—beginning on August 4, 1991—to dislodge Saddam Hussein's Iraqi forces from Kuwait produced a major foreign policy fracture among longtime Reagan supporters on the right. In the late summer of 1990, months before the start of the Gulf War, the *Wall Street Journal* and William Safire, conservative columnist of the *New York Times*, endorsed Bush's Middle East policy, while conservative pundits such as Patrick Buchanan, Jeane J. Kirkpatrick, and Robert Novak urged caution. Buchanan even spoke of a possible "quagmire" in the region, while ridiculing neoconservative Ben Wattenberg's desire to spread democracy across the globe as "global baloney." Arguing that Bush's reason for opposing Iraq's aggression was to aid Israel, he decried the world-view of a "geo-political conservative" like Safire, saying that "the old Cold Warriors, Catholics, and others who saw Communism as evil and a threat against our country will go back to our familiar point of view—let's tend to our own affairs."

As the Republican conservative movement began to experience "ideological gridlock," the Democrats continued to support deficit reduction as their key legislative priority, at a time when the economy was starting to go into a tailspin. In a period when poll data showed that Americans were more worried about the state of the economy and their future job prospects than the deficit, the Democratic party offered little or nothing substantive to inspire them to believe that it cared about their problems.

Yet there was little discussion of the economy during the midterm election of 1990. The possibility of war in the Middle East seemed to attract more national attention than the deepening recession. And so did the term limitation movement, which sought to impose restrictions on the time politicians could serve in office. This movement captured something of the growing national frustration with the failure of the political system to transcend the politics of deadlock and paralysis; as the 1990 election showed, however, it turned out to have more bark than bite. Established politicians were able to protect their turf from any such challenge. In addition, the power of incumbency also prevailed that election year, much to the relief of most sitting Democrats. Aided by contributions from corporate PACs, they retained their large majorities in Congress even though there was a decided falloff in the vote that many incumbents received that year.

Although the Democrats retained control of Congress, they had not yet found a way to transcend the politics of race. The Republicans continued to exploit the issue to their advantage in several key elections around the country. Senator Jesse Helms, for example, used the fear of racial quotas and affirmative action programs to defeat Harvey Gantt, a black Democrat, in a hotly contested battle in North Carolina. The same story was repeated in Alabama and California, where victorious Republican candidates for governor made less than subtle appeals for white votes. In Louisiana, David Duke, a onetime American Nazi and former Klansman, employed racial arguments against quotas and welfare to make a very strong run for the Senate against the conservative Democratic incumbent, Bennett Johnson.

These returns suggested that the racial cauldron was still boiling, much to the benefit of the Republican party. Such, then, was the context for the White House charge that the Democratic party supported "quota" legislation for the purpose of overturning a number of recent Supreme Court decisions, which had denied legal standing to various affirmative action programs. By attacking the Democrats in the name of equal opportunity and fair play for all citizens, the Bush administration, like the Reagan administration before it, sought the moral high ground by arrogating to itself traditional American values and standards.

Race had been a key to the GOP's ability to capture the White House in five out of the last six elections since 1968. Its political success also rested on its ability to produce a period of stable economic growth in the aftermath of the Carter failure. In addition, the Republicans were able to project a strong foreign policy, which made the Democrats appear weak and vacillating, lacking the toughness and tenacity to defend vital American interests in a dangerous world.

George Bush's Gulf War went far to reinforce that view for a brief period before domestic economic issues came back to erode his support among the voters. After mobilizing a strong domestic and international consensus to oppose Saddam Hussein's seizure of Kuwait, his triumph was so overwhelming that, following the "United Nations" victory over Iraqi forces in the winter of 1991, he attained a remarkable and unprecedented 90 percent approval in the polls. Consequently, his reelection in November 1992 seemed such a foregone conclusion that Democrat after Democrat, led by Congrooomon Richard Gephardt and Senators Albert Gore and Jay Rockefeller, decided not to seek the Democratic presidential nomination.

President Bush won the war in the Persian Gulf, but his battle with the American economy was far less rewarding. Although his overall approval rating stood at a staggering 90 percent in early 1991, only 43 percent supported his handling of domestic issues. And once the euphoria generated by the Gulf War began to fade, the deepening recession of 1990–92 eventually brought him down from the heights, as voters began to view his overall performance far more skeptically.

According to Michael Boskin, the chief White House economist, the recession that began in 1990 was caused by Hussein's invasion of Kuwait. In actuality, the downturn was already under way before the start of that war, caused mostly by the falling off in consumer demand and glutted markets, especially in the real estate sector. As unemployment reached 7.3 percent in early 1992, there was little evidence that any meaningful recovery was on the horizon, suggesting that the economy had become Bush's Achilles' heel. During his term in office, growth averaged only 2.5 percent in 1989, one percent in 1990, and a negative seventh-tenths of one percent in 1991. Such figures went far to confirm that the country was now in the grip of a far worse economic situation at home than at any time since the recession of 1981–82.

In a number of respects, the 1990–92 recession was unlike that of 1981–82, which is why Bush soon found himself in deep trouble with voters. For one thing, he had little or no fiscal policy at his disposal to cope with the downturn. The massive deficit, exacerbated by the S & L crisis, denied him the use of the key tool that Ronald Reagan employed via military Keynesianism to spend his way out of trouble in 1983 and 1984. In addition, the bite of the 1990 recession was such that many more white-collar jobs became redundant than in the early eighties. The rapid maturing of the service sector, in a period of widespread corporate cost cutting, now meant that there were fewer replacement jobs for middle management in such key sectors as insurance, real estate, and banking, or even for those employed at fast-food outlets inside the minimum wage economy.

Prospects for major improvement in the near future seemed poor. Available evidence suggested that white-collar service sector employment would grow at a rate of only 1.1 percent a year for the rest of the decade, as compared to 1.7 percent during the eighties. Many suburbanites were destined to face the grim reality that downward mobility was going to be as much a part of their lives as the 1981–82 recession had been for manufacturing workers living in the Rust Belt; they expressed deep disappointment both with Bush's domestic leadership and with his failure to acknowledge the impact of the recession on them.

As the optimism of the mid-eighties devolved into the growing despair and cynicism of the early nineties, the conservative coalition, which had helped to elect Ronald Reagan and George Bush, no longer had viable policies to cope with the structural changes affecting the American economy. Its free-market, supply-side-oriented economics was no solution for a slump produced partly by political factors resulting from a staunch ideological commitment to deregulation and tax cuts benefiting the wealthy. Thus, the combination of government inaction and globalization had produced the threat of an internal crisis going beyond the limits of the 1981–82 downturn. As one economist remarked, "The threat posed is an all-out private-sector credit contraction and asset price-deflation, accompanied by mounting corporate bankruptcies and bank failures."

Despite Bush's newly discovered vulnerability, the Democrats, in

1990–91, gave little indication that they were prepared to challenge the Republican presidential hegemony with either fresh policies or new ideas. Abiding by the deficit agreement of 1990, they largely ignored their own traditional commitments to provide help for those paying the biggest price for this latest business cycle reversal. In the face of growing unemployment and the spreading recession, the Democrats were only prepared to extend unemployment benefits beyond a certain period, a bill that Bush vetoed twice in 1991.

The failure of the Democrats to do very much to confront the recession of 1990–92 was consistent with their stance taken during the Carter years, at a time when they first surrendered fiscal policy to the Republicans. They had weakened their own once-strong base of support among working-class voters, on whom they were once heavily dependent, by going along with the politics of deficit reduction and the quest for balanced budgets. Consequently, the Democrats had little to say to those voters, as well as to many others who favored the restoration of an activist government to help them cope with growing health-care costs, environmental concerns, and job security. It was no surprise that self-identified Democrats from the lowest end of the socioeconomic scale dropped from 89 percent in 1987 to 57 per cent in 1990. This was the price that the national Democratic party seemed willing to pay in its eager pursuit of corporate PAC money and suburban voters, who, for the first time, would constitute a demographic majority of the electorate in 1992.

Yet the Democrats, along with a few moderate Republicans, could not completely ignore or forsake their longstanding ties to black Americans and other minority groups. Congress passed legislation designed to overturn recent Supreme Court decisions that had either struck down or very much weakened the legal standing of certain affirmative action programs. Bush at first argued that this bill was "quota"-biased, and he opposed it at every turn. But after denouncing David Duke, who was seeking to become the Republican governor of Louisiana by running a racially driven campaign against quotas and welfare programs, he eventually backed off and signed it into law in late 1991.

Bush's action, in this instance, clearly angered many Republican conservatives who felt betrayed by his sudden willingness to defend a process that both he and they had opposed for many years on both personal and ideological grounds. Patrick Buchanan later charged that George Bush, Ronald Reagan's loyal vice-president, no longer spoke for his brand of conservatism, and that the time had arrived to let Republican voters in the 1992 New Hampshire primary decide whether Bush's tax hike, his support of "quotas," and his "new world order" were what they wanted from a Republican president.

Much to Bush's deep chagrin and embarrassment, Buchanan's efforts paid off on one level. His candidacy revealed that 37 percent of Republican voters in New Hampshire were decidedly unhappy with Bush. Moreover, 30 to 40 percent in other primaries, even where Buchanan was not a factor, voted the same way, feeling that Bush lacked a compelling vision and program to inspire them as had Reagan. Still, it was too soon to say that Buchanan's political challenge to Bush marked the end of the Republican presidential hegemony of the eighties. But his campaign from the right, even though it was not strong enough to prevent Bush's renomination, was a good indication that the conservative coalition, which had elected both Ronald Reagan and George Bush president, was no longer the united force of an earlier period.

Whether the Democrats could benefit from the disarray in Republican ranks was an open question. Heading into the 1992 election, they were encouraged by the fact that Senator Harris Wofford had defeated Richard Thornburgh, Bush's former attorney general, in a hotly contested race in Pennsylvania to fill the unexpired term of the late John Heinz. Wofford had campaigned hard against the high cost of medical care, demanding some kind of public program to deal with the issue. Thornburgh foolishly defended the status quo and paid the price, losing a race in November 1991 that had been conceded to him in advance by virtually everyone but Wofford himself.

There were a number of Democrats, including Governor Bill Clinton of Arkansas, former senator Paul Tsongas of Massachusetts, and former governor Jerry Brown of California, who sought the party's 1992 presidential nomination in the aftermath of Wofford's success. Clinton, a leading member of the moderate Democratic Leadership Council, tried to create space for himself in the center of the party by endorsing tax cuts for the middle class. He also supported government-assisted programs to provide educational and job retraining for workers, hoping in this way to enhance both their marketable skills and their productivity. In addition, he was a strong proponent of workfare, which was an attempt to end the blight of welfare dependency. His approach would require those on welfare who were physically and mentally fit either to accept some degree of personal responsibility for finding work or to risk the prospect of losing their benefits.

Tsongas spoke for probusiness Democrats and many upper-middle-class suburbanites. He wanted to revitalize the American economy by stimulating investment in corporations through reducing the capital gains tax and relaxing antitrust laws. Lacking the money and votes to continue much beyond his victories in New Hampshire and Maryland, and his defeats in the South and the Midwest, Tsongas was eventually forced out of the race, leaving this spokesman for neoliberalism standing on the sidelines.

Jerry Brown, in his quest for the nomination, played the role of the outsider throwing darts at the political establishment. Voicing his concern that American democracy was in deep trouble, Brown argued that the political system itself had been corrupted by powerful forces whose campaign contributions had bought them influence and important connections far beyond the reach of the average American. He wanted to make major changes in the way government did its business so that the poor and forgotten were included in its calculations. In that vein, Brown proposed to overhaul the current tax system by replacing it with a flat tax at a 13 percent rate. But in the key New York primary, Clinton effectively demolished Brown's case for his tax, by showing that it would be even more regressive in practice than those tax laws currently on the books.

Clinton, like Jimmy Carter before him, failed to strike a resonant chord among large numbers of Democrats, who wanted someone else to move the economy out of its rut and to halt the country's spreading social decay. Despite persistent rumors about his private life and questions about his draft status during the Vietnam War, he still managed to secure the nomination by winning the key primary contests in all sections of the country. Well organized and vastly better funded than his fellow competitors, Clinton was a survivor. Whether he could put to rest questions about his character and still provide a viable domestic and international program to attract enough support to mount an effective challenge against a weakened George Bush would be determined by the campaign to come.

While Bush and Clinton awaited their respective nominations, the domestic political landscape was seemingly altered by a massive riot that occurred at the end of April in south-central Los Angeles, a downtrodden area inhabited by many poor blacks and Latinos. That riot, which resulted in the deaths of fifty-one people, injuries to several thousand more, and property damage estimated to be more than $700 million, was triggered by a jury decision freeing four Los Angeles policemen of the charge that they had used excessive force to restrain Rodney King, a black man in their custody.

As a consequence of the burning and mayhem associated with the Los Angeles riot, urban issues were forced back onto the national political agenda for the first time in many years. At the same time, a partisan debate erupted over who was responsible for creating the conditions that produced this riot. The White House charged that the failed social polices of the Great Society had been the chief culprit. Governor Clinton pointedly disagreed, saying that twelve successive years of Republican "denial and neglect" was the prime factor behind the explosion in south-central Los Angeles.

While each side was busily posturing, Kevin Phillips, no longer a conservative Republican strategist, offered his own analysis of the events in Los Angeles. He suggested that in the 1960s, "liberals were widely seen as having failed to deal with major questions of law enforcement, taxation, fiscal management, and the role of government, as well as race. They were repudiated, and the Republicans moved into a 25-year period of executive hegemony. Twelve years of Reagan and Bush has not cured the problems, either. It hasn't given us morning in America. It's produced more columns of smoke rising from our inner cities."

Such was the impact of the Los Angeles riot that according to a *New York Times*/CBS poll, a majority of Americans were now prepared to take fresh steps to address the nagging and often perplexing social and economic problems of the inner cities. But complicating matters was the lack of money. In 1992, many congressional Democrats were no more disposed to spend substantial sums on the cities for job creation and welfare reform than were the Republicans. In fact, like the Republicans, their chief legislative goal remained deficit reduction, which is why they rejected moves in April 1992 to transfer money saved from reduced military spending to domestic programs, and why some of them even supported an amendment to the Constitution requiring the federal government to balance its budget each and every year. Evidently, the ghost of Ronald Reagan continued to haunt many Democrats, who remained fearful that voters might yet hold them responsible for the nearly $400 billion federal deficit projected for fiscal year 1992.

Also, Ross Perot, an independent candidate for the presidency, tapped into the widespread feeling that the deficit problem was out of control and needed immediate attention. A Texas billionaire, Perot had long since emerged as a folk hero to large numbers of Americans. They identified with his efforts to find missing Americans in Vietnam, and they felt that his business acumen and outsider status would give him the clout to overcome the gridlock in Washington and thereby produce a balanced federal budget. At first, Perot did well in the polls, but after stories appeared in the media about his authoritarian manner and style, he suffered a fairly rapid decline in popular support. Withdrawing from the race in mid-summer, he provided Governor Clinton with an opportunity to pick up much-needed support from those many disappointed Perot supporters. (In early October, Perot renewed his bid for the White House; thanks to his strong performance in the three televised presidential debates, he found growing support across the country.)

Meanwhile, the state of the American economy provided Clinton and his running mate, Senator Albert Gore of Tennessee, with the key issue with which to challenge the conservative coalition that had put Ronald Reagan and George Bush in the White House. Whether they lived in the mostly white suburbs or the depressed inner cities, vast numbers of Americans were concerned that unemployment hovered around 7.5 percent, that medical costs continued to climb, and that the competitive strength and vitality of the domestic economy was no longer assured. Focusing on those assorted problems and issues, Clinton and Gore called for renewal of an activist government to cope with a stagnating economy by supporting governmental investments in the country's public infrastructure as one way of creating jobs and nurturing economic growth. But at the same time, they astutely ducked the charge that they were "tax-and-spend" liberals, which made it extremely difficult for the White House to mount an effective counterattack against them.

Clinton helped his cause by defining himself as a "third way" Democrat, neither of the left nor of the right. Declaring that he favored a fresh approach to solving the country's problems, one that did not rely on either the "trickle-down" economics of the Reagan-Bush era or the "tax-and-spend" policies of earlier Democratic nominees for the White House, he eschewed the label "liberal." Rather, he sought to position himself as a new-style centrist who refused to be locked into the social agenda or economic policies associated with either Senator Edward Kennedy or Jesse Jackson. That is, he called for reform of the welfare system; he favored the use of capital punishment; and he generally avoided discussing the growing financial, economic, and social plight of the cities, whose fate was of little interest to many suburban voters. Yet Clinton lined up with the defenders of *Roe v. Wade* and endorsed the Supreme Court's 5-4 vote on June 29, 1992, which upheld *Roe* in the important case of *Planned Parenthood of Southeastern Pennsylvania v. Casey.* (Ironically, in this instance, three of the five justices who voted in the majority had been appointed to the Court by either Reagan or Bush.)

George Bush, on the other hand, willingly embraced the political agenda of the Republican right. Seeking to protect his conservative base, he not only went along with pro-lifers at the Republican convention but stood his ground with them while they defended "family values." The Reverend Pat Robertson, leader of the Christian Coalition, accused Bill Clinton and his wife, Hillary, of working to undermine the traditional family. Marilyn Quayle, the wife of Vice-President Dan Quayle, observed that many baby boomers had not joined the counterculture or "dodged" the draft or trampled on values based on commitment, marriage, and fidelity. Such was GOP's attempt to resurrect the "social issue" with a new twist, which had worked so well for it in presidential elections going back to 1968.

Unfortunately for Bush, that cultural agenda no longer seemed relevant to the day-to-day psychological needs and economic concerns of millions of Americans, including many Reagan Democrats, who had been an integral part of the Reagan coalition as late as 1988. Worried about the state of the national economy and rising health care costs, they remained largely indifferent to the GOP pitch about family values. Moreover, they felt betrayed by Bush's tax hike of 1990. As one disgruntled former Bush supporter put it, "We have seen what Reagan and Bush have done. The butter's fallen off the biscuits."

Even before the election, other elements of the Reagan coalition were also upset with Bush. Some conservative intellectuals held him responsible for the political and ideological disintegration of the conservative movement, to which they had contributed years of effort. They were outraged that he had supported the tax hike of 1990 and signed the Civil Rights Act of 1991. They were also angered over his failure to deliver a knockout blow to Saddam Hussein after putting him on the ropes. Norman Podhoretz, a leading neoconservative publicist, was particularly scornful of Bush's presidency, suggesting that it was a political version of coitus interruptus. Bush "can't consummate anything," said Podhoretz. Edwin Feulner, president of the Heritage Foundation, stated that "our message" had been "sullied by a visionless White House pretending to be conservative." He opined that "conservatives supported George Bush and they got Michael Dukakis." Paul Weyrich, a luminary of the New Right, was also despondent about the future of conservatism, saying that "in the late seventies polls showed that the word 'conservative' had a positive image. As we come into the mid-nineties, that is no longer true. The Reagan-Bush coalition is dead. The movement that existed has been shattered. The principles it stood for are still true, but we need to find a way to reassert them."

These sentiments, expressed by individuals who helped to prepare the intellectual and ideological groundwork for the Reagan Revolution, reflected well the crisis of conservatism on the very eve of the 1992 presidential election. It was a crisis that had largely been precipitated by the end of the cold war. No longer could the Republicans successfully focus on foreign policy as a source of their strength and Democratic weakness. The demise of the Soviet Union also weakened the unity of the right, which had been predicated on a commonly shared anticommunism. With the loss of that political adhesive, foreign policy divisions resulting from the Gulf War appeared inside the conservative wing of the GOP; they could not readily be healed.

As Republicans sought to find a winning strategy, the Democrats stayed focused on the economy, which was far more important than foreign affairs or family values in deciding the political outcome in 1992. And their approach worked. A stagnant economy and a growing desire for change gave the Democrats control of both the White House and Congress for the first time in twelve years. Like 1980, people wanted a fresh approach and new faces to deal with the country's many problems. And like 1980, economic uncertainty and fear played the major role in determining who would win and who lose.

Having successfully exploited that situation, Clinton was able to build on the Dukakis foundation of 1988 by expanding his Democratic base to include parts of the South, including Georgia and Louisiana, plus key industrial states such as Illinois and Ohio. Receiving 43 percent of the popular vote and 370 votes in the electoral college, he produced his victory by bringing Reagan Democrats back into the fold, along with a plurality of women voters, and a majority of first-time voters. In addition, Clinton received significant support from those in the 18- to 24-year-old bracket as well as older Americans.

Losing candidate George Bush received only 37.5 percent of the popular vote and 168 votes in the electoral college, because he was unable to match in any respect the economic accomplishments of his immediate predecessor, including the reduction of the rate of inflation and the creation of millions of new jobs. Hence Bush was extremely vulnerable to the relentless attack that Clinton and Gore directed at him, and he had little or nothing to say that could offset it. Although he tried to defend family values in order to shore up his position on the Republican right, his views on abortion drove many moderate upper-middle-class Republican women into Clinton's camp. He also tried to focus on his victory in the Gulf War, but the country, facing serious problems at home, no longer cared. A victim of Reagan's deficit and his own tax hike, Bush was bereft of vision and the politics of growth. Consequently, when the American economy dramatically slowed down, his political fate was sealed. Yet, if the growth rate in the third quarter of 1992, which was reported after the election as amounting to a respectable 3.2 percent, had occurred much earlier in the year and had been sustained into November, Bush's chances of winning reelection would have been much improved.

Ross Perot received a staggering 19 percent of the total popular vote, winning at least 10 percent of all votes cast in every state but Mississippi. His support came mainly from independents or first-time voters who were fed up with the gridlock in Washington, and who wanted prompt action taken to balance the federal budget. According to political scientist Gerald Pomper, Perot voters constituted a "rootless" bloc that cut across all social, ideological, and geographic boundary lines, while they expressed an "unfocused discontent with the political system." Yet despite their anger with that "system," they did not appear to replicate the views of those passionate George Wallace voters, with their clearly focused resentments and hatreds, who helped to push American politics to the right for a generation.

As a result of Bush's defeat, Republicans were now in deep trouble. They lacked a popular leader or spokesman like Ronald Reagan, who could contain their schismatic tendencies, and they no longer had the cold war to help them forge a united front against the politics and policies of the new Democratic center. Furthermore, the social issue now seriously divided Republicans. For instance, someone like Jack Kemp, a putative candidate for the Republican nomination in 1996, had views on family values that were simply too libertarian for another possible Republican candidate, Pat Robertson, the chief spokesman for the Christian Coalition. Clearly, then, the GOP faced a future full of internal political turmoil and ideological conflict reminiscent of that which had dogged the Democrats in the twenty-five years preceding Clinton's election.

Clinton's victory made it appear as if the Democrats had finally discovered the political utility of moving back to the center on social issues, freeing them of their past attachment to a left-liberal social agenda that had spelled disaster for the party ever since the McGovern years. In order to prosper politically from this development, Clinton would have to produce evidence of a solid economic recovery and deficit reduction. This was no easy task, given both the constraints of a divided polity at home and the fact that the United States now had to function inside a highly competitive global economy. Thus, as the Clinton era dawned, it seemed clear that the old liberalism, as represented by Lyndon Johnson, and the laissez-faire politics of Ronald Reagan were now passé. Whether Clinton's third option, tied to his rejection of a "tax-and-spend" approach or of "trickle-down" economics, could provide a viable alternative to either of the other approaches is open to question.

Conclusion

The triumph of conservatism in the twenty-year period from 1968 to 1988 was rooted in the politics of race and the globalization of the American economy. As those two developments converged in the late seventies, they nearly destroyed what was left of the New Deal coalition. More specifically, once racial conflict spread from the South to the North after 1965, it quickly nationalized an issue that had long since prevented the South from moving beyond the politics of racial demagoguery. In the North, it included the issues of welfarism, forced busing, and affirmative action. In 1968, Richard Nixon exploited the racial backlash that coincided with the hostile reaction of millions of voters to the counterculture and the antiwar movement. His success that year marked the beginning of Republican presidential hegemony.

Republicans later benefited from the persistence of inflation and from a tax revolt. Those were the issues, along with race and culture, that led millions of angry lower-middle- and working-class white Americans to turn against the liberal establishment.

Social issues were important in the forging of the new Republican majority, but it was the state of the American economy that was the ultimate key to conservatism's success in 1980. The combination of inflation and globalization convinced many voters during the Carter years that the national Democratic party could no longer be trusted to provide responsible management of the national economy. If Jimmy Carter had vetoed the 1978 Revenue Act or had imposed price and wage controls on the economy, he would have earned the enmity of powerful business organizations such as the Business

Roundtable—but he would not have forsaken his party's traditional commitment to the Keynesian welfare state. Carter, a conservative Democrat, lacked the necessary political will or ideological resources to take such daring steps. Consequently, his inaction helped to foster and encourage the growing conservative movement.

When Ronald Reagan campaigned for the presidency in 1980, he represented an ideologically persuasive and well-funded conservative coalition, which included elements from business, various think tanks, and the religious right. After taking office, Reagan moved to implement his agenda with boldness and determination. What did he accomplish? With the help of Congress, he lowered taxes, weakened the regulatory state, reduced governmental services for the poor, and spent vast sums to rebuild the military. And he supported Paul Volcker's efforts to fight inflation via an induced recession. By 1983, Reagan's work was essentially completed, his goals having been reached.

In ideological terms, the various elements of Reagan's coalition were linked by a common commitment to diminished government. For conservatives, that was the heart of the matter. During the Carter years, a majority of Americans had turned against big government, seeing it as unworkable, inefficient, or delivering services that had nothing to do with them. That feeling was especially pronounced among middle-class voters, who resented paying taxes for a system that, they believed, supported "welfare chiselers." Thus, when Reagan promised to get government off the backs of the people, he struck the political equivalent of gold.

Given that mind-set, Reagan and his fellow free-market conservatives could not address the continuing erosion of American economic power in a global context. According to historian Paul Kennedy, Reagan actually *"exacerbated"* the situation he inherited from his predecessors. Reagan left the country in much worse financial shape in 1988 than was the case in 1980 by making the United States heavily dependent on foreign capital to fund its huge federal deficit and by converting it into the world's leading debtor nation. Though conservatives correctly argued that many Americans were better off as a result of Reagan's policies, Reaganomics had also produced mountains of debt and the likely prospect of much lower living standards for the middle class and the working poor. This was the price the American people were going to pay for policies that produced spectacular benefits for the top one percent of wealth holders and income earners and very little or nothing for the bottom 80 percent.

Fiscal realities, coupled with the conservative mood of the country, made it politically difficult for Democratic liberals to exploit that situation: they could not reconcile funding for new social programs with Reagan's huge deficits without raising taxes. Liberals also suffered from the near collapse of the American labor movement, which once had been the chief mobilizing force inside the old full employment coalition. In addition, they lacked a biracial national consensus to support a liberal policy agenda. Thus, Democrats had to cope with the reality that deficit reduction and the fear of new taxes, not new social programs for the cities, most concerned the critical suburban voter.

As old-fashioned welfare state liberalism suffered a tremendous beating in the eighties, a neoliberal ideology took hold inside the Democratic party, despite the efforts of Jesse Jackson to push the party in a left-liberal direction in both 1984 and 1988. Neoliberalism attracted such Democrats as Gary Hart, Michael Dukakis, and Bill Clinton, who sought to shift their party's focus solely from the problems and concerns of marginalized workers and the unemployed to the larger structural requirements of an American economy facing severe competition in the global marketplace.

The emergence of neoliberalism was a clear indication that the Democratic party no longer spoke with one voice about economic matters or anything else. At one time, the Democratic party was able to create a liberal voting majority out of diverse political elements because it offered broad social and economic programs that had wide appeal. But now millions of Americans viewed it as nothing more than a vehicle for special interest groups such as racial minorities and organized labor. Also, Democratic liberalism had become synonymous with Great Society social programs, which, according to neoconservative gospel, had wasted billions of taxpayer dollars in a "value-free" effort to provide uplift and support for lazy and ungrateful welfare recipients. Since this was the prevailing sentiment in the country, Republicans had little difficulty in tagging liberal Democrats invidiously as "tax-and-spend" Democrats.

By the early nineties, the conservative agenda that Ronald Reagan and George Bush had exploited to win the White House appeared increasingly out of touch with the new mood of the country. The ending of the cold war, as well as mounting domestic social and economic difficulties, had created a different set of concerns for large numbers of people, who were worried about the government's debt load, unemployment, and the country's faltering educational and health systems. They focused instead on problems that were not readily subject to the kind of divide-and-conquer politics practiced by such skilled Republican operatives as Lee Atwater. Hence, Republicans suddenly found themselves in a position much like that of the Democrats in 1980.

Conservatives had no such economic problems to overcome during their years of political growth. Since the late sixties, they had successfully made their way through the interstices of the American political system by focusing on anticommunism, big government spending policies, and the "rights revolution." Aided by liberalism's political and economic decline, they took power by promising to get the government off the backs of the people and to prevent the spread of communism. Now, however, their situation had changed because of a soured economy. Notwithstanding the salience of social issues, it again appeared that the economy was the crucial variable that determined who would win or lose national elections.

While conservatives faced the prospect of losing the White House in 1992, a number of liberal academics and journalists were at work exploring and analyzing a variety of social issues that neoconservatives such as Nathan Glazer had been discussing in print since the early seventies. Sociologists Christopher Jencks and William J. Wilson, for example, suggested that affirmative action programs did not necessarily provide the best answer for the various social problems plaguing poor black Americans. Journalists Thomas and Mary Edsall contended that the behavior of the urban underclass had contributed significantly to GOP presidential victories since 1968. Historian Fred Siegel argued that accountability and responsibility ought to go hand-in-hand with whatever largess the government distributed to welfare recipients. Coming from such credible liberal sources, these views represented an important reappraisal of social policy and behavior pertaining to race and class that would have been difficult to imagine in most liberal political and academic circles during the seventies and mid-eighties. In short, a new liberal consensus seemed to be emerging in the early nineties, which suggested that the era of "value-free" social policy on the left had come to an end. Such a reformulation appeared to be consistent with the views and values of mainstream opinion in the country, given the political fate of welfarism since the sixties.

At the same time, that budding consensus did not eschew state action with respect to social policy. Its goal was to overcome the stigma that had been attached to liberal social programs, namely, that they lacked moral content or that they focused only on race. As journalist E. J. Dionne points out, the recent discovery that "family values" are not the exclusive property of either liberals or conservatives provides the basis for reconstituting a new "vital center" on social policy. Here, possibly, was the means by which the fierce ideological wars between liberals and conservatives might yet be transcended.

During the 1992 campaign, Bill Clinton sought to bridge those ideological differences. Such was the challenge facing this Democratic nominee, who embodied a shrewd centrist awareness of the limits of liberalism and yet realized the need to forge a new national consensus to confront the damage to the public infrastructure wrought by the Reagan and Bush administrations. He struck a positive chord with the middle class by calling for the restoration of an activist government to cope with the manifold symptoms of social and economic decline. At the same time, he brought Reagan Democrats back into the fold by supporting "workfare" and capital punishment and by opposing affirmative action programs. Yet he also endorsed gay rights and feminist causes.

Nevertheless, the scarcity of political and economic resources made it questionable whether Clinton could still preserve that fragile coalition and initiate a program of reform. As America's first baby-boomer president, he was about to discover that there was no escaping the complex legacy of liberalism's past defeat or conservatism's recent political triumph.

BIBLIOGRAPHICAL ESSAY

Just as I began this project, a number of books and articles covering the rise of the conservative Republican era appeared in print. Much to my good fortune, that literature deepened my understanding of how and why Republicans won presidential elections for nearly a generation. The titles discussed below seek to highlight those particular books and articles that I found most important and useful in the construction of this synthesis. My hope is that this brief essay will inspire interested readers to examine further the rich and rapidly expanding literature on the subject of the rise and decline of the conservative order, 1968–1992.

General Surveys

A good starting point for the period under review is Fred Siegel's *Troubled Journey: From Pearl Harbor to Ronald Reagan* (New York: Hill & Wang, 1984), which connects the ethnocultural and racial conflicts of the sixties and seventies to the large-scale political and economic crisis that finally brought Ronald Reagan to power. Siegel's two essays, "Conservatism" and "Liberalism," in *The Reader's Companion to American History*, ed. Eric Foner and John Garraty (Boston: Houghton Mifflin, 1991), are especially insightful. Charles Morris's *A Time of Passion: America, 1960–1980* (New York: Penguin Books, 1986) provides a solid, though caustic, overview of the period, along with a first-class bibliographical essay. Godfrey Hodgson's *America in Our Time: From World War II to Nixon, What Happened and Why* (Garden City, N.Y.: Doubleday, 1976) is a brilliant interpretation by an able British journalist of the collapse of the liberal consensus. E. J. Dionne, Jr.'s, *Why Americans Hate Politics* (New York: Simon & Schuster, 1991) is a stimulating work that focuses on the political ideologies and social conflicts that ultimately produced gridlock in Washington. Thomas B. and Mary D. Edsall's *Chain Reaction: The Impact of Race, Rights, and Taxes on American Poli-*

tics (New York: W. W. Norton, 1991) is an important book that explains how and why the Republicans found the winning political combination they needed to capture and hold the presidency. David Vogel's *Fluctuating Fortunes: The Political Power of Business in America* (New York: Basic Books, 1989) explores well the background to and the consequences of the business mobilization of the late seventies. Vogel's book is required reading for all students interested in the recent history of business-government relations in the United States. Michael Barone brings together a wealth of information and sharp analysis in *Our Country: The Shaping of America from Roosevelt to Reagan* (New York: Free Press, 1990). Paul Gottfried and Thomas Fleming's *The Conservative Movement* (Boston: Twayne Publishers, 1988) surveys the ideas and politics of American conservatism since World War II. Walter Russell Mead's provocative *Mortal Splendor: The American Empire in Transition* (Boston: Houghton Mifflin, 1987) makes the case that the crisis of liberalism and the growth of conservatism are an outgrowth of an imperial order in decline. Gillian Peele integrates a wealth of useful material and sharp analysis in *Revival and Reaction: The Right in Contemporary America* (Oxford: Clarendon Press, 1984).

Introduction

Harold Myerson's perceptive essay "Why the Democrats Keep Losing," *Dissent* (Summer 1989): 308, is the source for his apt description of liberalism. Lee Atwater's remark is found in Edsall and Edsall's *Chain Reaction,* 221–22.

Chapter 1. The Politics of Culture and Class

David Chalmers's *And the Crooked Places Made Straight: The Struggle for Social Change in the 1960s* (Baltimore: Johns Hopkins University Press, 1991) is a fine synthesis of the sixties literature, replete with an outstanding bibliographical essay. Allen Matusow's *The Unraveling of America: A History of Liberalism in the 1960s* (New York: Harper & Row, 1984) is a an excellent account of the politics and problems associated with the emergence of Great Society liberalism. Michael Barone, in his magisterial *Our Country,* writes perceptively about the elections of 1968 and 1972. Edsall and Edsall's *Chain Reaction* explores the impact of racial politics and the "social issue" on American politics during the late sixties and early seventies. On the same subject, see Jonathan Rider's pithy essay "The Rise of the Silent Majority," in *The Rise And Fall of the New Deal Order: 1930–1980,* ed. Steve Fraser and Gary Gerstle (Princeton: Princeton University Press, 1989). A key book on the internal politics of the GOP is David Reinhard, *The Republican Right since 1945* (Lexington: University of Kentucky Press, 1983). Richard Nixon's comeback is captured well in Stephen Ambrose, *Nixon: The Triumph of a*

Politician, 1962–1972, vol. 2 (New York: Simon & Schuster, 1989). In that same vein, Herbert Parmet's *Richard Nixon and His America* (Boston: Little, Brown, 1990), is informative and insightful. The question of a political dealignment of the party system is raised in Walter Dean Burnham's *Critical Elections and the Mainsprings of American Politics* (New York: W. W. Norton, 1970). Kevin Phillips's brilliant reading of political trends is contained in *The Emerging Republican Majority* (New Rochelle, N.Y.: Arlington House, 1969). See also Richard Scammon and Ben Wattenburg, *The Real Majority* (New York: Berkley Medallion Books, 1972), whose good advice to stay focused on economic issues and avoid being identified with social issues many Democrats chose to ignore.

Hugh D. Graham's *Civil Rights and the Presidency: Race and Gender in American Politics, 1960–1972* (New York: Oxford University Press, 1992) is a superb case study of the relationship of the "rights revolution" to the evolving administrative state of the sixties and early seventies. It is a major work that deserves a wide readership. Vogel's *Fluctuating Fortunes* has excellent material on the regulatory politics and policies of the Johnson and Nixon years. David Calleo's *The Imperious Economy* (Cambridge: Harvard University Press, 1982) offers a searching analysis of the relationship of the American economy to the larger global system. Michael Harrington provides a social democratic perspective and much useful information about the state of the American economy during the late sixties and seventies in *Decade of Decision: The Crisis of the American System* (New York: Simon & Schuster, 1980). The emergence of a neoconservative current inside the Republican party is the focal point of A. James Reichley's *Conservatives in an Age of Change: The Nixon and Ford Administrations* (Washington, D.C.: Brookings Institution, 1981). Stanley Kutler's *The Wars of Watergate: The Last Crisis of Richard Nixon* (New York: Alfred A. Knopf, 1990) is an authoritative account of that event. Susan M. Hartmann's *From Margin to Mainstream: American Women and Politics since 1960* (New York: Alfred A. Knopf, 1989) is a concise survey of the politics of feminism and antifeminism.

Chapter 2. The Conservative Upsurge

Peter Carroll's *It Seemed Like Nothing Happened: America in the 1970s* (New Brunswick, N.J.: Rutgers University Press, 1990) is an excellent introduction to the political and social history of the 1970s. See Horst Brand's essay "Inflation and the Welfare State," *Dissent* (Winter 1975): 16–26, for a refutation of the neoconservative argument that a "tide of social demands" triggered inflation. Douglas Hibbs, in *The American Political Economy: Macroeconomics and Electoral Politics* (Cambridge: Harvard University Press, 1987), provides a well-researched analysis of inflation's impact on presidential politics during the Ford, Carter, and Reagan years. Horst Brand, in

"The Myth of a Capital Shortage," *Dissent* (Summer 1976): 298–306, rebuts William Simon's argument about a looming capital shortage. Michael Harrington's *The Next Left: The History of A Future* (New York: Henry Holt, 1986) is the source for the data on banking loans to the third world.

The key book on the Boston busing controversy is Ronald Formisano's *Boston against Busing: Race, Class, and Ethnicity in the 1960s and 1970s* (Chapel Hill: University of North Carolina Press, 1991). The deepening split between one-time liberal allies is spelled out in Jonathan Kaufman's *Broken Alliance: The Turbulent Time between Blacks and Jews in America* (New York: Charles Scribner's Sons, 1988). Earl Black and Merle Black's *Politics and Society in the South* (Cambridge: Harvard University Press, 1987) is a fine study that explores how and why the GOP established the basis for a presidential realignment in the South. James Sundquist's *Dynamics of the Party System: Alignment and Realignment of Political Parties in the United States*, rev. ed. (Washington, D.C.: Brookings Institution, 1983) is a trenchant study of presidential politics and the changing party system. See also Everett C. Ladd, Jr., with Charles D. Hadley, *Transformations of the American Party System* (New York: W. W. Norton, 1975), for a perceptive analysis of that same development.

Thomas Edsall's *The New Politics of Inequality* (New York: W. W. Norton, 1984) raises the point that business feared the direction that Congress would take in opposing its interests after 1974. Andrew Levison's *The Working Class Majority* (New York: Coward, McCann & Geoghegan, 1974) examines the social and ideological rift between organized labor and the McGovern wing of the Democratic party. Vogel's *Fluctuating Fortunes* takes note of an emerging business mobilization directed against the regulatory agenda of the public interest lobby.

The emerging New Right of the seventies is now the subject of growing scholarly interest. Jerome Himmelstein's *To the Right: The Transformation of American Conservatism* (Berkeley: University of California Press, 1990) is a well-researched study that breaks new ground, arguing that there was a fundamental continuity in beliefs and programs between the Old Right of the fifties and sixties and the New Right of the seventies. Kevin Phillips's *Post-Conservative America: People, Politics, and Ideology in a Time of Crisis* (New York: Random House, 1982) provides an informed and detailed account of seventies-style conservative populism. John Judis's *William F. Buckley, Jr.: Patron Saint of the Conservatives* (New York: Simon & Schuster, 1988) has much useful material about the life and times of a major cultural icon of American conservatism. William Rusher's *The Rise of the Right* (New York: William Morrow, 1984) is revealing about his own insider's role on the conservative right since the Goldwater years. The story of New Right's search for a presidential candidate in the 1974–76 period is well told in Alan Crawford's *Thunder on The Right: The "New Right" and the Politics of Resent-*

ment (New York: Pantheon Books, 1980). David Reinhard's *The Republican Right since 1945* is also a good source for internal Republican politics of this period.

Nicole Rae's *The Decline and Fall of the Liberal Republicans: From 1952 to the Present* (New York: Oxford University Press, 1989) shows how conservatives benefited from the new convention rules the GOP devised to compete more effectively with the Democrats. Mike Davis identifies key Reagan backers in *Prisoners of the American Dream* (London: Verso, 1986). Carroll's *It Seemed Like Nothing Happened* has good material on the 1976 campaign. Leo Ribuffo's "Is Poland a Soviet Satellite? Gerald Ford, the Sonnenfeldt Doctrine, and the Election of 1976," in his *Right Center Left: Essays in American History* (New Brunswick, N.J.: Rutgers University Press, 1992), 189–213, explores a key foreign policy issue of the 1976 campaign. E. J. Dionne's *Why Americans Hate Politics* provides an insightful analysis of how and why Jimmy Carter won the presidency in 1976. Norman Nie, Sidney Verba, and John Petrocik, in *The Changing American Voter*, enlarged ed. (Cambridge: Harvard University Press, 1979), examine voting patterns for that election year.

Chapter 3. Jimmy Carter and the Crisis of Liberalism

A good survey of the Carter presidency, which uses recently opened papers from the Carter Library, is Burton Kaufman's *The Presidency of James Earl Carter, Jr.* (Lawrence: University Press of Kansas, 1993). Vogel's *Fluctuating Fortunes* is key for tracing Carter's dealings with the public interest-labor coalition. Robert Lekachman's "Economic Policy," *Dissent* (Spring 1977): 116–17, notes the similarity in economic goals between Carter and Ford. James Savage's *Balanced Budgets and American Politics* (Ithaca: Cornell University Press, 1988) captures Carter's drift to the right on fiscal policy. Davis's *Prisoners of the American Dream* is highly critical of the tactics of labor's leadership. Michael Harrington's *Socialism: Past and Future* (New York: Arcade Publishing, 1989) analyzes the impact of globalization and declining productivity on the American economy. Thomas Ferguson and Joel Rogers, in *Right Turn: The Decline of the Democrats and the Future of American Politics* (New York: Hill & Wang, 1986), argue persuasively that globalization did much to weaken Carter by destroying the coalition that elected him. Thomas Edsall's "Congress Turns toward the Right," *Dissent* (Winter 1978): 12–18, is a perceptive examination of the shift then taking place in the ranks of House Democrats. Edsall's *The New Politics of Inequality* is a penetrating political and economic analysis of the origins and consequences of that shift.

Edsall and Edsall's *Chain Reaction* underscores liberalism's growing political difficulties during the seventies. Pursuant to the problems associated with legal liberalism, Fred Siegel notes that "a rights-based politics . . . has, for all its value, the effect of sharply dividing people." His insightful comments on the subject are found in "Back to the Future," *Telos* (Winter 1987–88): 157–61. For an elegant refinement of that same point, see also Siegel's essay "Liberalism" in *The Reader's Companion to American History.*

Hibbs's *The American Political Economy* is the best work on the inflationary developments of the Carter years and is the source for the Dionne quote.. Vogel's *Fluctuating Fortunes* spells out Carter's difficulties with Congress over tax, energy, and regulatory policies. Robert Lekachman's "Tax Nonsense, Conservative Style," *Dissent* (Winter 1979): 17–19, is the source for the data from *Business Week.* Peter Jenkins's *Mrs. Thatcher's Revolution: The Ending of the Socialist Era* (Cambridge: Harvard University Press, 1988) is an important work that explores the connection between inflation and the rise of Thatcherism. Kaufman's *The Presidency of James Earl Carter, Jr.* establishes the context for Carter's "crisis of confidence" speech. Harrington views the turbulent events of the late seventies as a reflection of a deepening crisis of the welfare state in "Why the Welfare State Breaks Down," *Dissent* (Winter 1980): 37–50. As the "malaise" of the late seventies gripped the country, it paved the way for a conservative mobilization of the electorate. Irving Howe probes the causes for that right turn in "The Right Menace," *New Republic* (September 8, 1978): 12–22, and "Thunder on the Right," *Dissent* (Winter 1979): 13–14. In *Thunder on the Right,* Alan Crawford narrates the story of how conservatives used the social issue to defeat liberal Democrats in several key Senate races.

William Greider's *Secrets of the Temple: How the Federal Reserve Runs the Country* (New York: Simon & Schuster, 1987) is the indispensable source for tracing Carter's dealings with Paul Volcker. Gaddis Smith's *Morality, Reason, and Power: American Diplomacy in the Carter Years* (New York: Hill & Wang, 1986) focuses on Carter's many foreign policy difficulties during the last two years of his presidency.

Chapter 4. The Triumph of Conservatism

George Nash's *The Conservative Intellectual Movement since 1945* (New York: Basic Books, 1976) is the authoritative work on this subject. Paul Gottfried and Thomas Fleming's *The Conservative Movement* is a concise and reliable overview of conservatism as a political and intellectual movement; it is particularly good on developments since the sixties. William Buckley, Jr., and Charles R. Kesler have put together an excellent anthology covering various aspects of conservative thought and ideology: see their *Keeping The Tablets: Modern American Conservative Thought* (New York: Harper & Row, 1988). Richard Viguerie's views are advanced in *The New Right: We're Ready to Lead* (Falls Church, Va.: Viguerie Co., 1980). Michael Kazin reviews the recent literature on conservatism in "The Grass-Roots Right: New Histories of U.S. Conservatism in the Twentieth Century," *American Historical Review* (February 1992): 136–55.

James D. Hunter's *Culture Wars: The Struggle To Define America* (New York: Basic Books, 1991) is an important work that did much to advance my understanding of the deep-rooted historical nature of the cultural conflicts of the seventies and eighties. Matthew Moen's *The Christian Right And Congress* (Tuscaloosa: University of Alabama Press, 1989) is a good study of the origins and politics of the religious right. See also Robert Liebman and Robert Wuthnow, eds., *The New Christian Right: Mobilization and Legitimation* (Hawthorne, N.Y.: Aldine, 1983). The incisive essays included in this volume by such scholars as James Guth, Jerome Himmelstein, Robert Liebman, and Robert Wuthnow, among others, are uniformly first-rate. Himmelstein's *To The Right* has very good material on the religious right. Ribuffo discusses the political significance of Jimmy Carter's religious beliefs in "God and Jimmy Carter," *Right Center Left: Essays In American History*. For a perceptive critique of the current literature dealing with religion's interaction with politics, see Ribuffo's "God and Contemporary Politics," *Journal of American History* (March 1993): 1515–33.

Peter Steinfels's *The Neoconservatives: The Men Who Are Changing American Politics* (New York: Simon & Schuster, 1979) remains the best source on the ideas of neoconservatism. Dionne provides a trenchant analysis of the politics of neoconservatism in *Why Americans Hate Politics*. Whether discussing the significance of Irving Kristol, the origins of supply-side economics, or the emergence of conservative think tanks, Sidney Blumenthal's *The Rise of the Counter-Establishment: From Conservative Ideology to Political Power* (New York: Harper & Row, 1988) is unfailingly perceptive. See also J. David Hoeveler, Jr.'s, *Watch on the Right: Conservative Intellectuals in the Reagan Era* (Madison: University of Wisconsin Press, 1991) for a portrait of Kristol as a leading neoconservative intellectual. Vogel's *Fluctuating Fortunes* is excellent on the business mobilization of the late seventies. Barry Sussman's *What Americans Really Think: And Why Our Politicians Pay No Attention* (New York: Pantheon Books, 1988) is full of interesting data on a variety of social and political issues, including what Americans thought about the welfare state.

Lou Cannon narrates Reagan's drive for the White House in his solidly researched *Reagan* (New York: G. P. Putnam's Sons, 1982). Vogel points to corporate concern about a Reagan candidacy in *Fluctuating Fortunes*. Michael Malbin's "The Convention, Platforms, and Issue Activists," in *The American Elections of 1980*, ed. Austin Ranney (Washington: American Enterprise Institute for Public Policy Research, 1981), is informative. Greider's *Secrets of the Temple* documents Paul Volcker's role in undermining Carter's hopes in 1980. James Savage's *Balanced Budgets and American Politics* analyzes the impact on fiscal policy of Carter's shift to the right. Horst Brand examines the administration's willingness to tolerate higher unemployment as a counter to inflation in "A Blow to the Welfare State: Carter's Policies and the Political Business Cycle," *Dissent* (Summer 1980): 273–78. Jerry Sander's *Peddlers of Crisis: The Committee on the Present Danger and the Politics of Containment* (Boston: South End Press, 1983) highlights the role played by Paul Nitze and others in helping to elect Reagan 1980. The use of coded racial messages in 1980 is explored in Edsall and Edsall's *Chain Reaction.* Rebecca Klatch's *Women of the New Right* (Philadelphia: Temple University Press, 1987) is an important study of a hitherto neglected topic.

Jack Germond and Julius Witcover provide a detailed journalistic account of the 1980 campaign in *Blue Smoke and Mirrors: How Reagan Won and Why Carter Lost the Election of 1980* (New York: Viking Press, 1981). Sundquist's *Dynamics of the Party System* is a sound appraisal of the 1980 election results. Edsall illuminates the role that money played in producing a conservative victory in *The New Politics of Inequality.* See also Walter Dean Burnham's penetrating essay "The 1980 Earthquake: Realignment, Reaction, or What?" in *The Hidden Election,* ed. Thomas Ferguson and Joel Rogers (New York: Pantheon Books, 1981). Dennis Wrong probes the political disaster that befell liberalism in "How Critical Is Our Condition: A Look at the Left and Liberal Left in America," *Dissent* (Fall 1981): 414–24.

Chapter 5. The Reagan Revolution

The starting point for the Reagan presidency is Lou Cannon's balanced and fair-minded *President Reagan: The Role of a Lifetime* (New York: Simon & Schuster, 1991). Alonzo Hamby provides a solid overview of the Reagan presidency in *Liberalism and Its Challengers: From F.D.R. to Bush,* 2d ed. (New York: Oxford University Press, 1992). Haynes Johnson's *Sleepwalking through History: America in the Reagan Years* (New York: W. W. Norton, 1991) is a perceptive journalistic account of Reagan's impact on American society during the eighties. Cannon's *Reagan* is indispensable for Reagan's pre-presidential years, as is Garry Wills's *Reagan's America: Innocents At Home* (Garden City: N.Y.: Doubleday, 1987). Martin Anderson's *Revolution* (New York: Harcourt Brace Jovanovich, 1988) is revealing about Reagan's economic views and policies during his first years as president. Hibbs discusses the 1981 Reagan tax cut and the battle over budget reconciliation in *The American Political Economy.* A superb account of the decade's political struggle over the budget deficits can be found in Joseph White's and Aaron Wildavsky's *The Deficit and the Public Interest: The Search for Responsible Budgeting in the 1980s* (Berkeley: University of California Press, 1991). Walter LaFeber cites the dollar figures for the projected military buildup contemplated by the Carter and Reagan administrations in *America, Russia, and the*

Cold War: 1945–1992, 7th ed. (New York: McGraw-Hill, 1993), 305.

Nathan Glazer's views on Reagan and the welfare state are found in *The Limits of Social Policy* (Cambridge: Harvard University Press, 1988). A work that Reagan extolled was George Gilder's *Wealth and Poverty* (New York: Basic Books, 1981). Another key book that provided a framework for Reagan administration thinking about social policy is Charles Murray's *Losing Ground: American Social Policy, 1950–1980* (New York: Basic Books, 1984). Harrington examines Murray's work in his *The Next Left*. Christopher Jencks challenges Murray's methodology in *Rethinking Social Policy: Race, Poverty, and the Underclass* (Cambridge: Harvard University Press, 1992). Michael Katz provides an excellent intellectual history of social policy since the sixties in *The Undeserving Poor: From the War on Poverty to the War on Welfare* (New York: Pantheon Books, 1989). David Stockman tells his story in *The Triumph of Politics: The Inside Story of the Reagan Revolution* (New York: Avon Books, 1987). Irving Howe's comments about Stockman are found in his blistering analysis of Reaganism, "The Spirit of the Times: Greed, Nostalgia, Ideology, and War Whoops," *Dissent* (Fall 1986): 413–25.

Davis, in *Prisoners of the American Dream*, focuses on labor's cataclysmic decline during the eighties. David Brody contrasts labor's fate in the United States with very different developments in Canada: see "The Breakdown of Labor's Social Contract," *Dissent* (Winter 1992): 32–41. Vogel's *Fluctuating Fortunes* provides an insightful discussion of what happened to the Reagan administration's efforts to deregulate the American economy. He also describes well the impact of the 1981–82 recession on key sectors of the American economy. Hibbs's *The American Political Economy* analyzes the economic recovery that preceded the 1984 election. Cannon's *President Reagan* provides the evidence of Reagan's support for Paul Volcker's "cold bath." Edsall's *The New Politics of Inequality* explores the fate of the congressional Democrats in the early eighties. See also Edsall's many penetrating journalistic pieces focusing on the politics of triumphant conservatism during the Reagan years in *Power and Money: Writing about Politics, 1971–1987* (New York: W. W. Norton, 1988).

Kevin Phillips documents the phenomenal transfer of wealth that flowed upward in the eighties in *The Politics of Rich and Poor: Wealth and the American Electorate in the Reagan Aftermath* (New York: Random House, 1991). Mark Levinson's data on family debt are found in *Dissent* (Spring 1989): 277–79. Edsall argues that a majority of American families in the eighties were not "net losers." See his review essay of Phillips's *The Politics of Rich and Poor*, which appeared in the *New Republic* (July 30 and August 6, 1990): 35–41.

Edsall and Edsall's *Chain Reaction* emphasizes the importance of race and the social issue as key factors that helped Reagan win reelection in 1984. The Democratic plight that year is captured well in Ferguson and Rogers's

Right Turn. Useful material on the Democrats is also found in Davis's *Prisoners of the American Dream*. Steven Gillon uses the newly available Mondale papers to good advantage in *The Democrats' Dilemma: Walter F. Mondale and the Liberal Legacy* (New York: Columbia University Press, 1992).

Chapter 6. Conservatism in Decline

Benjamin Ginsberg and Martin Shefter's *Politics by Other Means: The Declining Importance of Elections in America* (New York: Basic Books, 1990) illuminates the workings of the national political system in the eighties. For interesting data on the changing composition of the GOP, see Thomas Edsall's article in the *Washington Post*, July 12, 1992. Dionne's *Why Americans Hate Politics* has good material on the various cleavages inside the Republican party. For a penetrating look at the impact of Reaganomics on American society, see Horst Brand's "The Sour Fruits of Reaganomics," *Dissent* (Summer 1986): 263–71. White and Wildavsky offer a superior analysis of the political origins and significance of the Gramm-Rudman-Hollings Act in *The Deficit And The Public Interest*. See also the revealing discussion about GRH in Cannon's *President Reagan*. Vogel's *Fluctuating Fortunes* is good on the Tax Reform Act of 1986. For an insightful discussion of the end of tax progressivity, as well as the source for the Musgrave comment, see Horst Brand's "Not Much Reform in 'Tax Reform,'" *Dissent* (Fall 1986): 389–92.

Good material on the Social Security tax is found in the *New York Times*, January 14, 1990, 9; ibid., January 21, 1990, E4. Phillips examines the issue of American dependence on foreign investments in *The Politics of Rich and Poor*. LaFeber's *America, Russia, and the Cold War* is the source for the $60 billion figure in interest payments. Robert Kuttner explores the reasons for the high-priced American dollar of the eighties in his important work *The End of Laissez-Faire: National Purpose and the Global Economy after the Cold War* (New York: Alfred A. Knopf, 1991). For valuable data on export and import flows, along with wage rates in the manufacturing sector of the American economy, see the *New York Times*, November 14, 1991, 22. Bennett Harrison and Barry Bluestone's *The Great U-Turn: Corporate Restructuring and the Polarizing of America* (New York: Basic Books, 1990) is a major study of the transformed American economy of the Reagan years. See also Peter Passell's "Blue Collar Blues: Who Is to Blame?" *New York Times*, January 17, 1990, 26.

For Herbert Stein's astringent comments on Reaganomics, see the *New York Times*, September 2, 1988, 24. Lawrence Ritter's observations about the S & L crisis appear in a review article in the *New York Times Book Review*, September 22, 1991, 18. Reagan's comment about the significance of the S & L legislation is found in Lenny Glynn's "Who Really Made the S & L Mess?" *Dissent* (Spring 1991): 195–201. The Mark Russell quote is taken from Walter

Adams and James Brock's excellent *Dangerous Pursuits: Mergers and Acquisitions in the Age of Wall Street* (New York: Pantheon Books, 1989), 66. Also worth consulting is Horst Brand's "Merger Mania And Economic Decline," *Dissent* (Spring 1989): 137–42. For data regarding corporate indebtedness, see Robert Reich's "A Culture of Paper Tigers," *Dissent* (Winter 1990): 58–64.

Blumenthal notes the decline of the conservative right during the mid-eighties in *Pledging Allegiance*. John Judis points to the growing neoconservative disillusionment with Reagan's foreign policy in "Conservatism and the Price of Success," in *The Reagan Legacy*, ed. Sidney Blumenthal and Thomas Edsall (New York: Pantheon Books, 1988): 135–72. Judis mentions Podhoretz's comparison of Hitler's Germany with Gorbachev's Russia in *Dissent* (Winter 1989): 128.

Cannon points to Reagan's growing difficulties with the electorate in *President Reagan*. Edsall documents the closeness of the 1986 Senate returns in *Power and Money*, 327–330. For an illuminating discussion of the meaning of conservative egalitarianism, see Edsall and Edsall's *Chain Reaction*. Fred Siegel's quote is taken from "Conservative Opportunism, Liberal Cowardice," *Commonweal*, November 8, 1991, 642–47. Thomas and Mary Edsall examine racial politics in "Race," *Atlantic* (May 1991): 53–86. See also Cornell West's *Race Matters* (Boston: Beacon Press, 1993) for a brilliant critique of the racial views of both "liberal structuralists" and "conservative behaviorists." Cannon's *President Reagan* discusses the impact of the Iran-Contra affair on Reagan's standing with the public. Vogel captures the shift in public attitudes about the role of government after 1986 in *Fluctuating Fortunes*.

Blumenthal's *Pledging Allegiance* explores George Bush's efforts to hustle the religious right. Ethan Bronner's *Battle for Justice* (New York: W. W. Norton, 1990) looks at Robert Bork's failure to win Senate confirmation for a Supreme Court seat. Peter Peterson's pessimistic views about the state of the American economy appeared in "The Morning After," *Atlantic* (October 1987): 43–69. Phillips's *The Politics of Rich And Poor*, 75–76, is the source for his quote about the new plutocratic America. Robert Kuttner notes that Mario Cuomo escorted Peterson in "Reaganism, Liberalism, and the Democrats," *The Reagan Legacy*, 107–8.

Blumenthal's *Pledging Allegiance* is a good introduction to the 1988 presidential campaign. Not to be missed are Fred Siegel's excellent pieces discussing how and why Michael Dukakis, a quintessential "process" liberal, won the Democratic nomination and lost the election. See, for example, his "Campaign across Cultural Divides," *Commonweal* (March 11, 1988): 137–41; "Competing Elites," *Commonweal* (October 7, 1988): 523–25; and "Why Liberals Haven't Learned and Why," *Commonweal* (January 13, 1989): 16–20. Edsall and Edsall's *Chain Reaction* provides a trenchant explanation of how and why the GOP used the Willie Horton affair, along with the controversy surrounding the Pledge of Allegiance, to destroy Dukakis's bid for the presidency. Adam Clymer's piece in the *New York Times*, November 14, 1988, 14, is good on how the vote was distributed among different sections of the polity. Phillips examines Dukakis's failed populism in *The Politics of Rich and Poor*. Everett C. Ladd analyzes the changing national voting patterns in "The 1988 Election, Continuation of the Post-New Deal System," *Political Science Quarterly* (Spring 1989): 1–18. Harold Myerson probes the reasons for the continuing Democratic defeats in "Why the Democrats Keep Losing: The Abandonment of Economic Populism," *Dissent* (Summer 1989): 305–10. Senator Edward Kennedy's favorable comments about Reagan are found in the *New York Times*, March 7, 1989.

Blumenthal's *Pledging Allegiance* is the source for Bush's policy toward Moscow. The statement of the Business Roundtable appeared in the *New York Times*, May 11, 1990, C2. The source for the Democratic difficulties with the flag issue is the *New York Times*, June 26, 1989, 10; ibid., October 6, 1989. For the significance of the abortion issue in the 1989 election, see Dionne's *Why Americans Hate Politics*. Phillips's remark about the GOP's growing difficulties with its eighties agenda is found in the *New York Times*, November 24, 1989, 11. Poll data on Bush's standing in 1989, along with growing fears of a foreign takeover of American property, are taken from Kevin Phillips's article in the *Washington Post*, October 1, 1989. For data on income distribution and poverty, see Mark Levinson's "The Recession That Provoked No Response," *Dissent* (Fall 1991): 449–52, and "Our Economy Keeps Limping Along," *Dissent* (Winter 1992): 5–6. A good discussion of Moynihan's tax proposal is presented in the *New York Times*, January 14, 1990, 9. Data on the reduction of poverty among older Americans are found in Leonard Silk's article in the *New York Times*, May 12, 1989, 28. Kevin Phillips analyzes the reasons for the declining tax base of the cities and states in *Boiling Point: Democrats, Republicans, and the Decline of Middle-Class Prosperity* (New York: Random House, 1993). On that same point, see also Carol O'Cleireacain's "Costs of the New Federalism," *Dissent* (Spring 1991): 276–78. The Schumpeter quote appeared in the *Nation*, October 7, 1991, 396. For the nature of the first budget deal negotiated by the Democratic House leadership with the White House, see the *Washington Post*, October 14, 1990, C1, C2. White and Wildavsky provide an informed analysis of the 1990 budget act in *The Deficit and the Public Interest*.

The bitter debate among conservatives over Bush's Persian Gulf policy is described in the *New York Times*, September 6, 1990, A9; ibid., September 23, 1990. Thomas Edsall examines the 1990 election returns in the *Washington Post*, November 11, 1990, B4. Dionne looks at those same returns in *Why Americans Hate Politics*. The white-collar recession of 1990–91 is the focal point of an important analysis by Sylvia Nasar in the *New York Times*, August 24, 1991, 24. Phillips's *Boiling Point* documents the downward mobility of the middle class during the eighties and early nineties. For the impact of the Bush recession on various sectors of the American economy, see the *New York Times*, December 3, 1991; ibid., February 23, 1992.

Phillips's *Boiling Point* also provides a useful guide to the 1992 presidential campaign from an economic perspective. Poll data pertaining to the Los Angeles riot, along with Phillips's pointed remark about the Reagan-Bush legacy, are found in the *New York Times*, May 2, 1992, 9. Using the L.A. riot as a springboard for examining urban policy, Mike Davis presents a harsh and passionate indictment of government indifference to urban problems in "Who Killed Los Angeles?" *New Left Review* (January–February 1993): 3–28. For a shrewd and entertaining analysis of the 1992 Republican convention, see Garry Wills's "The Born-Again Republicans," *New York Review of Books*, September 24, 1992, 9–14. Joan Didion examines, with appropriate sarcasm, Clinton's march toward the Democratic nomination: see "Eye on the Prize," *New York Review of Books*, September 24, 1992, 57–66. For the details of the bitter conservative disillusionment with Bush, see Richard Brookhiser's "Gravedigger of the Revolution," *Atlantic* (October 1992): 70–78.

A comprehensive breakdown of the 1992 election returns was published in the *New York Times*, November 7, 1992, 8–13. Professor Gerald Pomper probed the character of the Ross Perot constituency at a symposium on the election at the University of Toronto, November 23, 1992. See also Everett Ladd's "The 1992 Vote for President Clinton: Another Brittle Mandate," *Political Science Quarterly* (Spring 1993): 1–28. Future GOP prospects and problems are examined in the *New York Times*, November 11, 1992, A16. For evidence that Clinton's victory did not put out the racial and ethnic fires raging inside the Democratic party, see Thomas Edsall, *Washington Post*, November 8, 1992, C1, C2. As Clinton took office, historian Paul Kennedy, writing from a global perspective, spelled out the many difficult social and economic problems facing him and the country as a result of the globalizing of the American economy: see "The American Prospect," *New York Review of Books*, March 4, 1993, 42–53.

Conclusion

Kennedy's pointed remark about Reagan appears in a useful symposium on the eighties that was published by *Commentary* (September 1990): 45. Dionne, in *Why Americans Hate Politics*, recognizes the emerging shift in liberal attitudes on social policy. Fred Siegel's views on welfare are cited by Thomas Edsall in the *Washington Post*, January 19, 1992, A14.

INDEX